Y0-DXD-705

Nations and Peoples

Italy

Italy

NINETTA JUCKER

with 34 illustrations and 2 maps

WALKER AND COMPANY

NEW YORK

In memory of F. P.

Library of Congress Catalog Card Number: 68–13988

First published in the United States of America in 1970 by the Walker Publishing Company, Inc.

Printed in Great Britain by Hazell, Watson and Viney Ltd, Aylesbury, Bucks.

Contents

1   The heritage

CONTEMPORARY ITALY is the product of 2,500 years of recorded history. Though some of the chapters are obscure it is an unbroken tale. The great fracture produced by the downfall of the Western Empire in the fifth century was less incisive in Italy than in the other Roman provinces of the west and the thread of cultural and ethnic continuity never completely snapped. The strands that make up that thread are many and various. From Neolithic times to the eleventh century AD peoples from all parts of the Mediterranean world have moved into Italy by land or sea. At the dawn of history these migrations were proceeding mainly in an east–west direction with a tendency for the newcomers to push the earlier inhabitants further west. There was a superimposing of languages and cultures, but as the Bronze Age gave way to iron the various inhabitants of Italy became established in the complex pattern of tribes and peoples known to the Romans, while the regional variations of their cultures developed under the stimulus of new contacts, giving birth in central Italy to the astonishing autochthonous civilization of the Etruscans. Italy was an ethnic jigsaw which puzzled the historians of antiquity and still causes dispute, but by the middle of the first century BC Rome had operated the most extraordinary synthesis, as unique in its way as the birth of the American nation in modern times.

A mosaic of clans and populations, some possessing an elaborate civilization of their own, others a more primitive culture, Greeks, Etruscans, Illyrians, Celts, Italic and pre-Italic peoples, some Indo-European, some not, were welded into a homogeneous latinized people, using the same language, worshipping the same gods, enjoying the same administrative institutions. This unity lasted some five hundred years, during which the inhabitants of peninsular Italy came as near as was possible in the ancient world to looking upon themselves as a nation in the modern sense. Only Sicily had been too deeply penetrated by Greek influence to partake in the process of fusion. The name of Italy, which had originally been used to designate the southernmost tip of Calabria, was gradually extended to the whole peninsula. At the end of the first century AD the elder Pliny, who was a native of Como in what had once been Cisalpine Gaul, could claim that Italy was the mother of all nations, with a mission to civilize mankind. Twelve hundred years later a similar notion recurs in the great medieval ideal, which inspired Dante, of a universal monarchy in which a politically united Italy would have a special place as the sacred garden of Christendom. But the spirit of imperial Rome was universal, not national, and the later emperors were seldom Italian-born, so that Italy lost its privileges and the city of Rome its prestige, and when the Western Empire collapsed in 476 AD the inhabitants of Italy had lost the radiant sense of spiritual unity and mission extolled by Pliny.

In the next four hundred years Italy was invaded successively by Visigoths, Ostrogoths, Lombards and Franks and intermittently raided by Saracens and Huns. Of all the Germanic peoples who settled there the Lombards were the most primitive and fierce and their penetration went deeper than any other. For two centuries (568–775) they subjected Italy to bloody anarchy and misrule from which the Church and its bishops emerged as the real centres of power in the country. At last the Franks invaded Italy at the call of the Pope. They were the most civilized of the Germanic folk and in contact with them Italy participated in the great Romance culture of south-west Europe. Their domination lasted nearly two centuries during which the Papacy laid the foundations of its temporal power. Until it finally collapsed in 1870 that power depended in great measure on the protection of the rulers of France.

An ethnic and cultural experience of great importance for Sicily was the Saracen domination, which lasted from 878 to 1090. Moorish civilization was nearing its zenith at the time and Sicily became once more a centre of economic and intellectual importance as it had been twelve hundred years earlier with the Greeks. Poetry and agriculture flourished there under the Moors and to this day cultivated Sicilians look back with nostalgia to that supposedly happy time, whose image burns the brighter for the darkness that followed.

With the arrival of the Normans in southern Italy and Sicily the ethnic picture of the Italian nation is more or less complete. Such complex origins are remarkable even for a Mediterranean country and it is not surprising that the Italians developed a concept of nationhood in which the factors of language and culture are infinitely more important than the idea of race. One of Italy's most illustrious historians, Federico Chabod, believed that this concept coloured their attitude to the problem of national unity during the great struggle for independence in the nineteenth century, differentiating it from the contemporary German approach. While the Germans were seeking a lost tribal unity and perfection, for the Italians liberty and independence meant the acquisition of a totally new status, in which they were to be a free nation on equal terms with other free peoples.

Like other nations born from the matrix of latinized Europe, the Italians emerged with their own language and literature and an embryonic national conscience between the tenth and the twelfth centuries. By the end of the thirteenth theirs was the leading culture in Europe and it remained so for the entire period of transition from medieval to modern times. This culture and this national awareness developed within well-defined geographical frontiers and, in different circumstances, would almost certainly have given birth to a political nation at the beginning of our modern era when France, Britain and Spain emerged as the prototypes of the European nation-state. Contemporary Italians wondered why they too could not become a political nation and found the short answer in the temporal power of the Popes. Machiavelli and Guicciardini, writing in the early sixteenth century, complained that the Papacy was forever calling now on the French kings now on the Emperor to promote its territorial interests, and by so doing had made Italy the battle-ground of foreign powers and prevented the amalgamation or the federation of the Italian states. This was true enough but another reason for the division of Italy was the fact that during the long struggle between the Pope and Emperor, when the Papacy was fighting for spiritual as well as material power, both sides courted the towns and so favoured the development in north and central Italy of virtually independent and finally sovereign city-states.

The importance of the Italian Communes for the future of Europe can hardly be overstressed. They provided the indispensable political context for the birth of the great intellectual movement of the Renaissance. The towns were small, close-knit communities whose institutions and economy resembled those of the ancient city-states and they developed an ethos which was consciously modelled on that of Athens, or, as with Florence, on republican Rome. An educated lay élite sprang up and found in city life the stimulus for a critical and philological reappraisal of the classics which was the starting point of the New Learning. The early Italian humanists were deeply interested in the business and theory of government. Many of them held municipal office and it was in action more than in contemplation that they developed the spirit of critical curiosity and the methods of research that were to supply the key to modern science and, when applied to the Gospels, gave birth to the Protestant Reform.

But the city-state, which had proved such a powerful intellectual stimulant, was politically a dead-end. By the middle of the sixteenth century the north Italian cities, with the exception of Venice, had ceased to be more or less aristocratic republics and had come under the government of local rulers. The change was not regretted at first, for the princes were all Italians and great protectors of the arts. This was the most prosperous and magnificent period of Italian history and from it the Italians have derived certain habits of mind. Theirs is a society which attaches great importance to letters, one in which it is easier to overcome disadvantages of birth or fortune than to live down lacunae in a classical education. From their Renaissance the Italians have retained an overwhelming respect for learning and for creative intelligence, a quality they now call *ingegno* but which in Machiavelli's day was called *virtù*. They esteem it more than moral excellence, and its cult accounts for a common Italian fallacy, the belief that genius is a racial attribute of the Italic temperament (in contrast to the self-discipline and other alleged social virtues of the Anglo-Saxons). Most Italians accept without discussion the proposition that they are a 'race' of individualists.

Italian society of the Renaissance was keenly aware of its intellectual superiority over its neighbours and the tendency to distinguish between Italy and barbary, or non-Italy, survives, not as a nationalistic or moralistic discrimination but as a sort of intellectual or cultural *apartheid*. Italians find it hard to believe that foreigners educated according to a different curriculum from their own, no matter what their scientific or technical achievements, can be really 'civilized'. So too the populace will never believe that members of the non-Catholic religious sects can be Christians though in colloquial Italian the word Christian is synonymous with a human being. This intellectual provincialism is slowly dying out among the young but it is still very tenacious in the teaching profession, both in the schools and universities, and is a serious obstacle to any modernizing reform of methods and curricula as well as to international co-operation and exchange.

From the last phase of the Renaissance modern Italians have retained a fundamentally static and pessimistic attitude towards human nature and society. The joyous belief in man's power and his place in the universe which sparked off the great movement did not survive the disasters that overtook Italy in the sixteenth century. Machiavelli was convinced that, in any state, the majority of citizens will never desire the common good unless this is imposed upon them by the laws of an enlightened and magnanimous prince; Guicciardini came to believe that in times of trouble (and Italy was to be in trouble most of the time for the next four hundred years) the wise man should withdraw from public life and cultivate his particular interests. The generations that followed retained the pessimism without the stoicism of the Renaissance thinkers and adapted to the conditions of their day. Even in the nineteenth century Italians never fully embraced the contemporary religion of progress.

The city-states were too weak and disunited to preserve their independence when the Pope and the Emperor came to terms, and with the Treaty of Cateau-Cambrésis in 1559 the greater part of Italy (with the exception of the Venetian Republic and the Papal States) passed under Imperial, that is Spanish and later Austrian, domination. The society whose learning, art and manners had been the model for the rest of Europe foundered slowly in a blaze of artistic and intellectual glory, its financial domination undermined by the influx of American silver, its commercial supremacy challenged by the new sea-faring powers on the Atlantic and the new patterns of world trade. But the final blow to the Renaissance way of life in Italy came from its own heart and centre when the Papacy, which had been the economic and spiritual fulcrum of that society, made the choice imposed upon it by the Reformation, gave up the enlightened religious tolerance inspired by Erasmus, and revived the medieval theology of the scholastics, based on the fear of Hell and the persecution of original thought. This theology was revived in a more sophisticated form, the better to inculcate the principle of obedience, and was imposed in Italy with techniques of persuasion and intimidation unknown to the Middle Ages but which became the model for the ideological brainwashing of our own time.

The Counter-Reformation with its mysticism and its austerity is ultimately the product of Spanish culture rather than Italian, though it had strong native roots in Venetia. In a sense it was a popular movement, a reaction against the too rarefied aristocratic intellectualism of the Renaissance, but its application in Italy was first and foremost a political move. It produced as vigorous a crop of saints there as in France and Spain but its repressive anti-intellectual character was always paramount, overshadowing its charitable, missionary side. Although the Roman Inquisition was generally less fanatical than the Spanish, it succeeded in crushing intellectual speculation for the sake of religious conformity. It made Galileo retract the theory of Copernicus on the movement of planets and it burned Giordano Bruno, the father of immanentist philosophy, at the stake. In Naples the Spanish Inquisition kept Tommaso Campanella, the author of a famous Utopia,[1] in prison for thirty years. In one way or another, the Inquisition silenced the greatest spirits of the age and discouraged their disciples. It was the beginning of a long period of spiritual and intellectual stagnation and of the most fearful economic regression. The Church, with its trained cadres of Jesuits and Dominicans, its pedagogues and its directors of conscience, came to exercise enormous influence on the education of the nobility, which became docile and conformist, content to find its private pleasures not too severely censured. At the same time the populace, which was severely tried during those terrible decades of famine and pestilence when the population in the big towns dropped by more than a third, found succour in the great hospitals and charities founded by the religious orders.

In 1559 southern Italy, Sicily and Sardinia became part of a Mediterranean system controlled from Madrid and exploited by the Spanish kings for their war against the Turks. The economic consequences for the south were disastrous. Spanish rule was not only oppressive, it was inefficient and corrupt and provided neither security nor justice. Though a host of lawyers sprang up to deal with incessant litigation, strong men took the law into their own hands and those who could not get justice became brigands or left the country to serve the Turks. Italians look on the two and a half centuries of Spanish domination as their second Dark Age. It left southern Italy with a society of negligent landowners possessing vast estates, of landless peasants crushed by debts, of intriguing lawyers and bigoted priests, of outlaws protected by the peasantry from fear or sympathy, of the secret societies, the Mafia and the Camorra.

Together the Counter-Reformation and the Spanish hegemony left Italy politically dismembered and culturally stifled, but they taught the Italians some defensive techniques. The emphasis on the family as the only social unit to provide security and satisfaction dates from these years. The family became a cult. Its interests and prestige took precedence of every other form of loyalty and prevented the municipal patriotism of the Italians from developing into a sense of community. The family became a defensive unit first and foremost in relation to the state, which was foreign and hostile, the enemy of the poor and the legitimate prey of the strong. To cheat it was no dishonour. To avoid taxes or military service or any of the other vexations imposed by governments was praiseworthy, and this bred indifference or even contempt for the civic duties and social responsibilities men usually accept when they are masters in their own land. One may wonder why these attitudes have survived so long in Italy after the achievement of national unity. Perhaps one answer is that, consciously or not, they have been encouraged by the Church. More than in most Catholic countries welfare and education in Italy have been the business of the Church, which still fulfils many of the duties of the state. Moreover for a long time after unification the Church was hostile to the state and took no interest in the behaviour of the citizens as such. To avoid taxes was not a matter for confession and is hardly so today when the Church itself is fighting to preserve its own immunity from the dividends tax.

Whatever the cause, these antisocial attitudes survive and have been studied by American sociologists and historians. In 1958 Edwin Banfield drew the following conclusions from a study of Italian society in the south: (1) A short-term material advantage is the only reason for taking an interest in public affairs; (2) public affairs concern officials and not private citizens; (3) whichever group is in power is presumed to be greedy and corrupt; (4) there is no relationship between abstract principles and everyday behaviour; (5) a request based on public interest rather than personal advantage is presumed to be fraudulent; (6) officials and professional people look on their position as a weapon to be used for their own advantage.

The Dark Age ended at last in 1713 when Italy passed from Spanish to Austrian rule and came under the influence of the Enlightenment. This had the effect of arousing a new sort of intellectual patriotism among Italians. People were mortified by the state to which Italian letters had declined since the Renaissance and began to reappraise Italy's original contribution to the ideas which were now rebounding upon her from northern Europe. The result was a new awareness among Italians from all parts of the country of their common cultural heritage and the desire to restore the prestige of Italian learning. This intellectual reawakening was the preliminary to the revival of the national idea and its first expression was a movement to revivify the language. The word *Risorgimento* enters Italian usage at this time. At first it denoted the revival of Italian letters and science and the consequent upsurge of national feeling among the intellectuals. Later it was extended to cover the entire period of the political struggle for national unity and independence.

The Italian Risorgimento was born of the moral ferment and the political upheavals produced by the French Revolution, and for all its singularity the movement has an inseparable European context. It was something more than a mere struggle for national unity and independence on the part of a people who had never been united politically but had in common an extraordinarily rich cultural heritage. Most of the great leaders of the Risorgimento had spent years in exile. They did not envisage the achievement of national unity, freedom and independence as an end in itself but as the means to the moral elevation of the Italians and, thanks to the 'civilizing mission' of Italy, of all mankind (by which, in the nineteenth century, they meant the peoples of Europe, particularly those under Austrian or Turkish rule). The idea that political unity must imply a spiritual mission was the common denominator between the many contra-dictory ideologies which combined to produce the Risorgimento. The movement was fed by the most diverse trends: centralizing and decentralizing, federalist and confederalist, monarchist and republi-can, catholic and anti-clerical. It embraced various economic philosophies and covered class and dynastic interests which now seem to have little connection with the moral elevation of mankind.

For sixty years and more this movement, with all its conflicts and contradictions, its heroism and its naïveté, provided an emotional climate of extraordinary fervour such as no other western nation has lived through for any comparable period of time. With the achievement of unity, followed inevitably by disappointment, the various ideologies, which had joined forces in pursuit of the grand design, became disentangled. Yet none of them quite withered away and in the hundred years that followed, now one ideological trend, now another, has been uppermost; for the final choice between a centralized and a decentralized government, as between a Catholic and a non-clerical concept of the state, has still to be made.

2 A nation is born

ON 17 MARCH 1861 King Victor Emmanuel of Piedmont was proclaimed King of Italy by the grace of God and the will of the nation. A hundred years after the event we know that united Italy was to be a going concern but at the time neither the European powers nor the Italians themselves were at all certain that the new kingdom would prove viable. It had inherent weaknesses and two invidious neighbours who might turn them to account. It had come into being against the will of the Pope. Pius IX would not acknowledge its existence and excommunicated the King. His successors kept up real, and later formal, hostility for over fifty years and it was only towards the end of the 1880's that Italians began to feel reasonably certain that neither France nor Austria would help the Pope to recover his temporal power. Another great weakness was the fact that the kingdom's finances were in disorder, while its government had to embark without delay on a programme of public works – railway building in particular – to give the country a minimum of structural unity. Italy's component parts were not only disconnected but extremely diverse and each had its own administrative and legal traditions. The only common denominator between them had been the cultural heritage of an elite. Even the language, in preference to dialect, was spoken habitually by very few. Most serious of all, though not so obvious to contemporaries, was the great cleavage – partly historical, partly climatic and economic – which divided the former kingdom of Naples from the rest of the country. The inhabitants of the south belonged to a civilization (or its aftermath) which harked back to the south-eastern part of the Mediterranean. Those of northern and central Italy looked northwards and forwards towards Europe. This northern orientation was accentuated, during the years which saw the birth of the Italian kingdom, by the opening of the new railway tunnels through the Alps.

United Italy was in the hands of the liberals, divided between Right and Left. Neither group was an organized party in the modern sense but, for a short time, the two sides faced each other in a straightforward parliamentary contest between government and opposition. The Right, which governed from 1861 to 1876, was dominated by Piedmontese and Tuscan landowners and stood for constitutional monarchy and a limited suffrage based on wealth. The Left in theory still preferred a republic based on universal suffrage, but it was divided between the diehards like Mazzini who refused to be reconciled to the monarchy and those, far more numerous, who were willing to accept the new regime. Among these converts were some outstanding personalities from the south. Both Right and Left were uncertain at first whether to prefer a centralized government or some sort of decentralization. For many years (as late as 1946) radicals were attracted by the ideas of Carlo Cattaneo, who had wanted united Italy to be a democratic federation of self-governing regions. Stefano Jacini and Marco Minghetti on the Right also preferred decentralization. In fact, however, centralization was sprung upon the country from Turin before anyone had time to object.

During the plebiscites of 1859 and 1860 the illiterate masses had been asked to vote, but in the new Italian state the franchise was regulated by a tax qualification taken over from Piedmont. Some five hundred thousand Italians out of twenty-two million[1] were enfranchised but only about half of them used their vote. Devout catholics kept aloof from politics and afterwards followed the injunction of Pius IX neither to vote nor to stand for election.[2] Their estrangement enabled the liberals of Right and Left to dominate parliament for four decades. The franchise was extended in 1882 to those who could read and write but the peasants had no direct say in politics until the introduction of manhood suffrage in 1912. Since at first neither the catholics nor the peasantry felt any particular loyalty to the Italian state it was fortunate that political power remained in the hands of the minority who believed in parliamentary government and had fought for the national idea. Right and Left had on the whole a high sense of their duty to defend the hard-won benefits of unity, independence, and constitutional freedom. As time went by, however, they adopted an exclusive attitude towards other sections of the population and outstanding liberal philosophers like Benedetto Croce and Gaetano Mosca came to believe and to teach that liberalism and democracy were a contradiction in terms, or so at least their elaborate thinking was construed by their disciples.

Between 1861 and 1870 the Piedmontese imposed upon the rest of Italy their own centralized prefectorial system of government, their military tradition, and their bureaucratic machine. Charles Albert's Statute of 1848[3] became the constitution of the realm, a loose constitution which was to remain in force, throughout sixty years of parliamentary democracy and twenty years of dictatorship, until the downfall of the monarchy in 1946. The spirit of the statute was liberal but the powers invested in the monarch made it possible, when circumstances changed, to adopt a non-liberal reading. The King was head of the executive and ministers were responsible to him. If necessary he could govern by decree. Thanks to the prestige of Cavour and the liberals of his generation, with their immense admiration for British usage, Italian governments in practice required a majority in the Chamber. Members of the Senate were appointed for life by the King, but the Senate's powers were limited. The Savoy monarchs were more jealous of their military than their political prerogatives. The King was commander-in-chief of all the armed forces, with power to make treaties of peace, alliance, and trade. The foreign minister was often his personal nominee, and the ministers of war and the navy were usually generals and admirals who owed special obedience to the King. In times of trouble it was customary for the monarch to appoint a general as premier. A Court party dominated by the military surrounded the throne, perpetuating (in the words of Professor Mack Smith) 'the dangerous notion that War was a gentlemanly and desirable occupation.'

The Italian peninsula

The linch-pin of the Piedmontese-Italian system of government was the prefect. Appointed by the King and answerable to the minister of the interior, the prefect was the highest authority in the province and acted as the government's watch-dog over the local councils with powers to suspend the mayor and elected councillors. Until the introduction of manhood suffrage, liberal premiers used the prefects to put government pressure on candidates and voters in order to 'make' elections. Later, during the years of fascist violence in the early 1920's, the 'co-operation' of the prefects was an indispensable factor in the advent of the fascist régime. Italian liberals have never been quite happy about the prefects, and Luigi Einaudi, before becoming President of the Republic in 1948, proposed abolishing the office. The desire to get rid of a potential instrument of arbitrary power has always been one of the motives behind the drive towards regional autonomy. Today, after twenty years of restored democracy, the issue is still unresolved.

In the 1860's Italians were given to believe that Piedmontese centralization was a temporary measure justified by the danger of foreign attack and by disaffection in the south. The outbreak of brigandage on the scale of civil war in the former kingdom of Naples disconcerted the stoutest upholders of regional de-centralization. Neither the Right nor the Left understood the social reasons for this unrest, but they saw that the Pope and the exiled Bourbons were blowing on the coals and sending foreign mercenaries to officer the rebel bands. Right and Left agreed that the Italian state must uphold its authority by force, for the problem uppermost in liberal minds was the fear that chronic rebellion in the south might make the European powers doubt the solidity of the new kingdom.

The 'war' against the brigands raged over southern Italy for five years. Over a hundred thousand regular troops were sent to put down the rising. Siege tactics were used, and scores of villages were sacked and burnt. Reprisals on both sides were carried out with ferocity and at least three thousand summary executions took place. The misery and destruction entailed were immense. In 1860 Garibaldi had marched his Thousand through Sicily and Calabria on the crest of a classical peasant's revolt. He mistook it for a patriotic rising and for a brief season transformed it into one. On his own authority he promised the peasants land and cheap food. The central government removed him with alacrity. The peasants received no land, and food prices promptly rose. Unification spelt new taxes and conscription, which was a novelty for the south and caused thousands of fugitives from military service to swell the armed bands. A harsh law of 1863 and military operations brought the south to heel in 1865 (a rebellion in Palermo was put down the following year), but the price paid in terms of national harmony and integration was enormous. From the very beginning, north and south gave up the attempt to understand each other and the southern peasants drew back in mute suspicion of the Italian state and its laws.

Public works, administrative reorganization and heavy military expenditure saddled united Italy with an enormous deficit. Railway and industrial development were going forward with the help of foreign loans, and to the men in government no task seemed more urgent than to build up the country's financial credit. Quintino Sella was the outstanding personality in the governments of the Right. Years later he recalled how the ambassador of a foreign power had offered to internationalize Italy's debt. To accept this would have declassed the Italian kingdom from the status of a European power to the semi-colonial condition of Egypt. Right and Left agreed that the budget must be balanced but they differed about what taxes should be raised for the purpose. The Left, in opposition, and supported by the new industrial and commercial classes, wanted a land tax and other forms of direct taxation, but the Right insisted on shifting the burden from land onto the consumer. This policy reached a climax with the unpopular grist tax (on the grinding of corn) which Sella was obliged to restore in 1869. The tax produced hardship and in the riots which followed two hundred and fifty people were killed and four thousand landed in jail.

Sella and Francesco Ferrara, the ministers responsible for restoring the nation's finances, were men of high principle according to their nineteenth-century lights. They believed that confidence in the currency must be maintained, if necessary without regard for the

21

social cost. But they started a tradition in the management of Italian finance which was revived after World War II and has tended in the long run to accentuate rather than resolve the eternal dilemma of the national economy with its ever-widening gap between north and south, between industry and agriculture, between rich and poor. It is fair, however, to remember that in Sella's day the incidence of indirect taxes was not proportionally as high as it became later and that Sella himself counterbalanced his fiscal severity by imposing the strictest economy on military spending.

Another method employed to meet the financial crisis of the 1860's was the confiscation and sale of ecclesiastical lands. This produced a fall in land values and the results were disappointing. The shortage of capital was such that the land, which was sold in small lots with a view to promoting peasant ownership, fell into the hands of speculators. This happened on a wide scale in the south. In the end the peasants lost their grazing rights and other perquisites, with the disappearance of the last vestiges of common land, while the new owners proved tougher landlords than the monasteries. In fact the liberals destroyed the last traces of a medieval economy in the south and centre without putting a new system in its place. But they succeeded in balancing the budget in 1876, the year in which the Right fell from power. Two features of the Italian economy were established during those years: a tax system which came to rely more and more on indirect taxes and put the greatest burden on the poor, and the progressive impoverishment of agriculture as the middle classes began to buy land for security or prestige but not to capitalize it.

The outstanding problem for government during the first decades of unity was to find a *modus vivendi* with the Papacy. Cavour had dreamed of a grand reconciliation in which the Roman Catholic religion and the spirit of liberalism were to join hands for the illumination and comfort of mankind. This was to be Italy's great mission. Cavour imagined that the Pope himself would see how the loss of his temporal power must favour the spiritual growth and influence of the Roman Catholic faith. The idea that religion would gain in purity and fervour from the institution of a 'Free Church in a Free

State' was shared by many honest catholics among the liberals but in fact a hundred years were to pass before a Pope – Paul VI – came to admit that the Church had actually gained from the loss of its temporal power. Formal reconciliation between the Papacy and the Italian state was achieved eventually by the dictator Mussolini in 1929. In 1866 Carlo Boncompagni noted with astonishing acumen that sooner or later reconciliation was bound to come. What he feared was that it might be the work of men who had small regard for liberal principles.

To expect a speedy reconciliation with the Papacy in the 1860's was unrealistic and indeed naïve for one of the first acts of government was to abrogate the concordats negotiated before unification by the separate Italian states. The anticlerical legislation of Piedmont – the main cause of Pius IX's aversion to the Savoy monarchy – was extended to the whole of Italy. Convents and other religious corporations were deprived of their property. Seminarists were made liable for military service and civil marriage alone was recognized by the state. Some financial vexations were justified on the ground that many religious foundations had been endowed for purposes of charity and education, charges which, in theory, now devolved on the state.

Pius IX answered by showering anathema on the liberals and all their works. He refused to negotiate with Cavour's emissaries in 1861 and would not recognize Italian sovereignty over the annexed territories, which he claimed to regard as stolen goods. In 1862 he declared he could not be free without his temporal powers and in 1864 he issued the famous *Syllabus of Errors*,[4] denouncing all the principles of liberalism with special emphasis on freedom of discussion, of conscience and of the press. Behind this intransigence was a grand design of the Jesuits to accentuate the centralized, authoritarian character of the government of the Church. The new policy, which tended to diminish the authority of the bishops and to strengthen the influence of the Roman Curia, was consolidated by the Vatican Council of 1869–70 which approved the dogma of papal infallibility. In the years that followed, the conflict between the liberal governing class and the Papacy became embittered and generated a new sort of shrill and often vulgar anticlericalism very different from the high-minded secularism of Cavour. This lampooning anticlerical spirit spread from the radical to the socialist press and bedevilled Italian politics for several decades.

In 1871 the Italian Parliament passed a law to establish the rights and privileges of the Pope. Pius IX and his successors refused to recognize the 'Law of Guarantees'.[5] They claimed to be prisoners in the Vatican and would not touch the annuity conceded by the Italian state. For a long time they did not admit the legal existence of united Italy. The King himself was excommunicate and in 1874 the Pope's *non expedit* enjoined catholics neither to stand for Parliament nor to vote. This ostracism was softened in course of time but the process was very slow and meanwhile the prolonged estrangement of the catholics prevented the growth of a strong conservative party in Italy and so influenced the type of parliamentary government which developed there between 1870 and 1915.

Cavour and his contemporaries had imagined a Parliament which would work like the British, with two parties contending for power, but the 'dialogue' between Right and Left petered out after 1876. The Right never returned to government for any length of time and the ideological and political difference between the two sides gradually became blurred. Both represented the liberal bourgeoisie. The Left became more conservative in office than it had been in opposition and it used the advantage of being in government to 'manage' elections. The Italian Chamber, like the French, was a semicircle in which a man could change his allegiance without 'crossing the floor'. Majorities were carved from the centre and gravitated upon this or that personality. No great political issues divided the House and men were won over by taking care of their personal interests. Cabinets were also formed by calling in men who had previously been in opposition and the whole shifting system of government became known as *trasformismo*.

Many Italians were shocked to see their Parliament dominated by personal rivalries and petty disputes. They felt that something was amiss but failed to understand that they had adopted institutions modelled partly on the British system, partly on the French,[6] and in either case taken from countries in a more advanced stage of economic and social evolution. In some respects Italian politics recalled the British parliaments of the eighteenth century but with an important difference: behind the intrigues and the jobbery in Italy there was no solid social structure. Rural Italy, with its characteristic share-cropping system of farming, had neither a squirearchy nor a class of yeomen farmers. Absentee landlords, harsh bailiffs and debt-ridden peasants were the rule in the south. The ill-balance of this society was at least one cause of the weakness of Italian democracy. But the fundamental reason for the failure to develop a two-party system alternating between government and opposition was the fact that a large proportion of the community – the catholics at first and later the socialists – were hostile to the very idea of parliamentary government and refused to accept its rules. A similar dilemma was to emerge with the Communist party when democracy was restored to Italy after World War II. *Trasformismo* developed in the 1880's as a substitute for the two-party system of government and gave rise to a series of so-called parliamentary dictators. Agostino Depretis, Francesco Crispi and Giovanni Giolitti in turn commanded a personal majority in Parliament between 1876 and 1913.

A dispute between Tuscans and Piedmontese split the Right in 1876 and put an end to the political domination of the landowners. Italians were later to look back with regret to the administration of these austere gentlemen, for never again was Italy to be governed by men of such personal standing. But the Right had made itself unpopular in the country by its taxes, while the Court was impatient of its tight-fisted control on military spending and its unadventurous approach to foreign affairs.

The advent of the Left under Depretis was considered a 'parliamentary revolution' and caused the same sort of excitement as the admission of the socialists into government in our own day. It seemed to mark the beginning of a new era, for the leaders of the Left were men who had followed Mazzini and Garibaldi and had taken part in the heroic and romantic adventures of the Risorgimento. Depretis was not the most outstanding figure among them but the choice fell on him as a northerner unquestionably loyal to the King. His programme was mildly progressive. It included a more equitable distribution of taxes, greater local autonomy, free and obligatory elementary schools and some measures of relief for the poor. The hated grist tax was removed in 1880 but the effect was spoiled when government, hard pressed for money, introduced a consumer tax in 1882.

The Left's most audacious reform was an extension of the franchise on a mixed basis of income and elementary schooling. This enlarged the electorate from 600,000 to over two million in 1882, but the bar on illiteracy meant that southern constituencies had fewer voters than the north and were thus more easily 'managed' by government, the more so as a large proportion of voters in the south were government employees. Inevitably, prime ministers came to rely more and more for their majorities on deputies from the south. The corrupting and demoralizing effects of the system, which reached its climax under Giolitti, were denounced with tremendous vehemence by Gaetano Salvemini and other southern radicals, to the extent that their indictment helped to discredit Parliament as an institution, but their anger was justified, for political morals in the south were permanently damaged and in parts of Sicily, to this day, the electoral machine is controlled by the Mafia.

One effect of the franchise reform was to thrust a wedge between the illiterate peasants in the south, who had no representatives in Parliament, and the industrial workers of the north, some of whom could read and write. This was to affect the future evolution of socialism in Italy, and later of communism, for the socialist leaders tended to pay more attention to the workers than to the rural masses. Neither Salvemini nor the communist leader Antonio Gramsci, for all their prestige, were able to overcome this breach.

The advent of the Left produced no remarkable changes in the political life of the country but it was none the less a landmark in the story of the spiritual changes that were taking place in Italy, as in the rest of Europe, after the cataclysm of 1870. The downfall of Napoleon III shook the generation that had been reared on the romantic idealism of the first part of the nineteenth century. Both Mazzini's ideal of universal brotherhood and Cavour's equally idealistic concept of a consortium of civilized nations were destroyed, and many in Italy as well as France bewailed the end of European civilization.

The exit of Napoleon and the triumph of Bismarck presented Europe with a new model, the man of blood and iron, and a new set of values. Hitherto Italians had thought of the nation as a historically moulded cultural and spiritual entity. They now began to accept the Germanic concept of the nation as a natural organism, God's gift to the ethnic group, obeying its own natural laws. This idea owed much to Charles Darwin's doctrine of the survival of the fittest, which greatly influenced the positivist thinkers in Germany. The new ideas penetrated Italy together with admiration for German science, German industrial progress and German military strength. During the Risorgimento France had been the model for Italian nationalists. Spiritual rivalry with France determined Gioberti's[7] and Mazzini's ideas of Italian primacy or an Italian mission. A love-hate relationship with France coloured the whole story down to the last episode during the Franco-Prussian war, when Garibaldi characteristically set off, unaided, with a handful of volunteers, to fight for the French Republic,[8] while the Italian government decided, after a brief heart-searching, to remain neutral lest the new kingdom itself should be wiped out as an appendix of Napoleon's empire.

The new ideology glorifying the ideas of military strength and moral regeneration through war was particularly acceptable at Court where King Humbert I, his imperious Queen, and his military entourage all believed that the monarch should look out for some warlike exploit in which to win prestige.

The Right had never believed that Italy should try her strength in the race for colonies, though less on moral than on practical grounds, but the Left had a more adventurous spirit and soon gave up the policy of 'clean hands' proclaimed in 1878 at the Congress of Berlin.[9] The new philosophy of strength snapped the link that had kept the idea of nationhood anchored, during the Risorgimento, to the idea of freedom. Marco Minghetti, an old liberal of the Right, put it sadly: 'We believed in justice and freedom. Today men believe in strength and numbers.'

The story of united Italy is essentially the tale of how the nation fell into the abyss of fascism and how it came out again. In this drama the time factor is important. Unity came to Italy just as Europe was entering the spiral of industrial protectionism, colonial expansion and the arms race. These phenomena were connected with the philosophy of power. Like the other European countries, Italy embraced the policies which seemed dictated by the spirit of the times, but the country's economic and social structure were not strong enough to sustain them. *Realpolitik* was unrealistic for Italy. Bismarck put the matter crudely in his celebrated phrase: 'The Italians have a large appetite and such poor teeth'.

In pursuit of national greatness Italy entered the Triple Alliance with Germany and Austria, embarked on some ill-fated adventures in Africa and engaged in a disastrous tariff war with France. These policies are usually associated with the curious personality of Francesco Crispi, whom Italians mistook briefly for the strong man they were expecting in the image of Bismarck, but in fact their origin goes back somewhat earlier.

Italy entered the arms race as soon as she had balanced her budget in 1876. The first care was to build up the navy, which in 1878 had the two biggest ironclads in the world. This was largely the work of King Humbert and his minister for the navy, Admiral Brin, who promoted a big ordnance factory at Terni. The British firm of Armstrong was encouraged to build a naval shipyard and cannon foundry at Pozzuoli and more naval engineering developed at Venice. Thanks to subsidized shipbuilding the Italian fleet became for a short time the third in the world for tonnage. With this military orientation heavy industry grew up under state patronage and behind protective tariffs and was neither efficient nor economical. Protection was theorized as a necessity because Italy lacked steel and coal, and the protective spirit spread to other industries.

Most of Italy's celebrated firms were founded in the two decades following unification. The Pirelli rubber factory dates from 1872. The Edison hydro-electric installations began to spread over northern Italy in 1884 and the Montecatini chemical industry was founded in 1888.[10] In those pioneer decades the big captains of industry, who were more forceful personalities than the politicians, established a special relationshp between industry and the state with a view to obtaining the monopoly of the home market. Knowing by instinct where to put the pressures, they became newspaper owners. *Il Corriere della Sera*, *La Stampa*, *Il Messaggero* and other important journals were founded during those years. At a time when party funds did not exist, deputies (and high-ranking officials) received financial aid from industry and the banks. These pressures were aimed to persuade government and the public that for the sake of national prestige public money should be spent on armaments and that tariffs should be raised to protect costly industries. Thus in Italy the birth of big industry and modern journalism coincided with the genesis of nationalist propaganda. This was not a purely Italian experience. Jingoism was rife in Britain at the time and France and Germany were equally nationalistic. Italy went with the stream but failed to realize that although she had the ships and the guns to compete with the others at the start, they were costing her more than she could afford.

Inevitably Italian diplomacy found itself keeping pace with this industrial-military build-up. Years earlier, when Napoleon III suggested that Italy and France might partition Tunisia, the Italian government declined, but the foreign minister of the day privately expressed the hope that 'the Turkish tart would not be served until Italy was ready to move up from the lower table to the high.'[11] Later governments still refused to become involved in Africa but a change of attitude set in when France established a protectorate in Tunisia in 1881. This seemed an unfriendly act to Italians, who had a big settlement there. Southerners looked on Tunisia as a geographical extension of Sicily and even Mazzini preached that Italian influence should return where the Roman eagles once triumphed over Carthage.

Italy was piqued and in 1882 Depretis carried the country into the Triple Alliance with Germany and Austria to break down Italy's diplomatic isolation. This was a reversal of the policy of non-alignment, or freedom to change sides, which had been the diplomatic strength of the House of Savoy. The real architect of the alliance was in fact Bismarck, who wanted to put a wedge between Italy and France. The alliance altered Italy's relations with Austria. Italian governments could no longer countenance agitation for the 'recovery' of the so-called 'unredeemed' territories of Trentino and Trieste. In compensation they could assume that Austria would not intervene to restore the temporal power of the Pope, but in fact this danger was probably more imaginary than real in 1882, whereas irredentism was a living sentiment.

For this reason, but also because the treaty was an agreement with conservative anti-liberal powers, the Triple Alliance never took hold of the Italian imagination although it was renewed five times and lasted for thirty years. Like the Nato alignment adopted after World War II, it was intended to influence home politics quite as much as international relations. The aim was to enlist catholic support for a conservative resistance to growing labour unrest (just as Nato was embraced with a view to keeping Italian communists in check). But whereas the Nato alliance was to become a way of life in Italy, the *Triplice* remained sterile. It failed to appease the catholics since Leo XIII was afraid that any softening towards the Italian government would cause the Papacy to lose face with other catholic powers. As a diplomatic instrument it was never put to the test, but its frequent renewal caused Italians to put too much confidence in the elaborate system of territorial swapping and compensation it was meant to sanction. When the system broke down after World War I the Italians were taken by surprise. During the first years of its existence the Triple Alliance encouraged Italian governments to prefer a policy of colonial expansion in unfriendly competition with France to the 'redemption' of Trentino and Trieste.

When France and Britain set up their protectorates in Tunisia and Egypt, Italy fell back on the Red Sea as 'the key to the Mediterranean'. In 1882 a trading settlement at Assab, founded with government help by a Genoese shipping company in 1869, was declared an Italian possession. Massawa, evacuated by the Khedive, was appropriated in 1885. Both were to serve as bases for colonial expansion in East Africa. Italy counted on the friendly presence of Britain in the Sudan but chose the moment of General Gordon's defeat for an ill-timed excursion into the highlands of Ethiopia, where five hundred Italians perished in the massacre at Dogali in 1887. In that year Depretis died and Italy, under Francesco Crispi, began its most unhappy experience of government before Mussolini. Crispi[12] had been the brain behind Garibaldi's famous exploit of 1860 but from a romantic jacobin he had turned into an aggressive nationalist, enamoured of Bismarck's Germany and moved by an irrational dislike of France. In government he was authoritarian, rash and incompetent. In 1889 he made Italy sign the Treaty of Uccialli with the Negus Menelik, which the Italians read as an invitation to set up a protectorate over Ethiopia. They occupied Asmara and founded a colony called Eritrea on the Red Sea. Menelik and his chieftains did not accept this reading of the Treaty of Uccialli but Crispi thought their subjection would be as easy as Garibaldi's conquest of Naples. He did not tell Parliament what he was about for he knew it would not grant him funds. The war was not popular in Italy except with the generals and the Court, for finances were strained and people doubted the utility of a colony on the Red Sea. All the same, when Crispi was out of office between 1891 and 1893, his successors felt unable to pull out of Ethiopia altogether though they cut down military funds. This enraged the generals and alarmed the King. Those were years of economic crisis and social disquiet and the Court believed a strong army might be needed to put down disorder at home, while the generals claimed the army would become demoralized if it were not given a chance to fight.

In 1893 Crispi was recalled and the Ethiopian campaign was resumed but misunderstandings developed between the government and General Baratieri and the upshot was a crushing and totally unexpected defeat at Adowa in 1896. Italy's first attempt to conquer Ethiopia cost the country eight thousand lives and some five hundred million lire. The colony of Eritrea remained, but the name of Adowa was to ring as harshly in Italian ears as Caporetto twenty years later. United Italy was born in an age of power worship and these defeats saddled the nation with a dangerous inferiority complex.

Italian industry grew up in the years of the great trade depression between 1873 and 1895 (when the price spiral set in motion by the discovery of Californian and Australian gold ceased until gold was found in the Transvaal). During those years wheat prices in Europe slumped as steam navigation brought cheap grains from North America. The depression affected Italy in a special way by accentuating the economic imbalance between north and south. Italian industry was already concentrating in the north thanks to the railway links with France and Bavaria. Milan, Turin and Genoa formed an industrial triangle and a centre of economic and hence political pressure which governments could not easily resist. When the steel and cotton industries asked for protective tariffs the government appointed a commission to examine the implications. The commission found that tariffs would hurt agriculture, particularly the oil and wine sectors which were already hit by the depression. But the wheat growers, some of whom owned big estates in the south, made common cause with the northern industrialists in demanding tariffs. So began the 'unholy alliance' denounced by Salvemini between the big industrial and land-owning interests, both of them owners of influential newspapers, which was later to play a part in the advent of fascism.

Protection became the declared policy of government in 1887 with the application of a general tariff, extended in the agricultural sector to rice, wheat and sugar. A year later Italy denounced its trade agreement with France. The economic effects of this policy were disastrous. France had been Italy's chief trading partner and the biggest foreign investor in Italian development (albeit with a view to favouring French industry rather than Italian). Crispi believed the French would accept the new Italian tariffs but the French ministry was as anti-Italian as Crispi was anti-French. Italian exports to France dropped by two-thirds and the French ceased to import Italian wines and silk. The wine producers of Sicily and Apulia, who had recently planted new vineyards, were ruined and henceforth investors were to fight shy of agricultural improvements in the south. Italy's rural economy was further damaged by the encouragement to put unsuitable land under grain. French investors reacted to Crispi's challenge by selling their Italian securities and so helping to precipitate the series of bank failures culminating in the great crash of the Banca Romana in 1893.

One catastrophe followed another throughout the nineties. The bank smash coincided with a rising in Sicily and another in Lumigiana. Then came the humiliating defeat of the Italians at Adowa followed by the tumults of 1898 in Milan, which gave the bourgeoisie its biggest scare before the great fright of 1919 to 1920. To contemporaries it looked as though the whole liberal system of government was tottering to a fall. The budget was in deficit again with too much spending on armaments. Social conditions had deteriorated since unification as the agrarian crisis, made worse by the government's protectionist policy, pushed the rural population into the towns and started the flow of emigration overseas.[13] Taxation and tariffs sent up food prices, hitting the basic diet of the poor. Pellagra, a deficiency disease, spread throughout north-east Italy while malaria increased in the south, where the reckless cutting down of trees led to the formation of mosquito swamps. Everywhere, in the rush to build ships and railway tracks, Italy's forests had been hacked down without thought for future erosion. Though the population was rising fast, public health was far from satisfactory. In overcrowded, insanitary Naples a cholera epidemic killed fifty-five thousand people in the eighties. Trachoma and typhoid were endemic in the south while the incidence of TB among the sulphur miners of Sicily was close on a hundred per cent.

While rural Italy was making its first violent contact with industrial civilization the towns were growing rapidly in a fever of uncontrolled speculation and graft. Government buildings were going up in Rome, where the population rose from 220,000 to 450,000 in two decades. Milan, Turin, Naples and the other big towns were growing equally fast. Fortunes were made rapidly with so much spending on public works, and the building boom was a free-for-all in which the banks were tempted to take part (thus diverting funds from productive investment in industry and agriculture). United Italy still had six regional banks of issue, each of which cultivated its personal relations with the men in government (on the pattern of the political system of the day). The banks over-reached themselves, issuing paper currency beyond the safety level, while Crispi abolished the legal restrictions on credit. The great crash of the Banca Romana led to a big political scandal which caused Giolitti to resign in 1893 though subsequent revelations showed that Crispi was even more to blame. It was largely to drown the noise of this scandal, which dragged on until 1895, that Crispi played up social unrest at home and re-launched the Ethiopian campaign.

3   Liberal decline

As INDUSTRY GREW the workers began to organize themselves in Italy as elsewhere, but the special features of the economy caused Italian socialism to develop along lines of its own. At first the workers found themselves at the mercy of a triumphant middle class which thought that liberalism meant the right to exploit the terms of supply and demand of labour as of everything else. Later the consolidation of a small, non-expanding, highly protected home market for industry allowed organized industrial workers to enjoy some of the privileges of protection, so that they came to form a working-class aristocracy. Moreover the fact that workers and employers had a common interest in obtaining government protection for a particular industry gave substance to the corporativist theories elaborated first by the catholic sociologists and afterwards by the fascists. At the same time the widening gap between north and south exasperated rural discontent and led to recurrent outbursts of violence on lines more similar to the traditional type of peasants' revolt than to a modern labour movement. These outbursts were as little understood by the socialist theorists in Milan as by the liberal ministers in Rome and prevented the peasants and industrial workers from forming a permanent united front in spite of the many episodes of impassioned and sometimes heroic co-operation. Socialism developed as a protective sectarian movement in defence of industrial workers, and the rift between industrial and rural labour was accentuated by the fact that, for a long time after unification, the Church took up the cause of the peasantry against the liberal state.

As in other industrial countries, the workers' movement grew out of the mutual aid societies which appeared soon after 1848 in Piedmont. Lombardy followed and the societies were soon flanked by the more combative 'resistance' leagues, precursors of the trade unions.

Farm labourers as well as industrial workers formed their leagues, which became powerful in certain rural areas, particularly Emilia where farming was conducted on a basis of hired labour. The leagues raised strike funds and organized recurrent labour agitation in the Po Valley, notably during the strikes of 1884–5. In addition to its leagues, fraternities, co-operatives and workers' banks, the Italian labour movement, in imitation of the French, set up Labour Chambers, an institution unknown to the workers in Britain or the USA. The Chambers served as regional headquarters for workers belonging to different organizations and, like the leagues, were not at first identified with theoretical socialism.

Socialist ideas entered Italy from France during the 1850's. In that decade Carlo Pisacane stands out as the first Italian revolutionary to see his country's history in terms of the class struggle. In the sixties the workers' movement was dominated by Mazzini, who impressed it with his republicanism. But Mazzini refused to countenance the notion of class struggle, which would destroy the sacred unity of the nation, and his influence waned after 1870 when his hostility to the Paris Commune lost him the sympathy of the workers. This went to Garibaldi, whose active intervention in France and impassioned appeal for social justice and universal brotherhood pleased the workers who wanted national unity to be crowned by the advent of a Social Republic.

Meanwhile marxist propaganda was pouring in after the First International had been set up in London in 1864. Marxism contrasted with the ideas of the Russian anarchist Bakunin, who had settled in Italy and became the outstanding figure in the Italian labour movement in the early seventies. Bakunin's ideas harked back to eighteenth-century egalitarianism. He wanted the peasants to own the land (whereas the marxists taught that land should belong to the community) and thought the only form of government necessary was the local commune. His teaching galvanized the land-hungry peasants in the Romagna, where he founded a local anarchist tradition which is alive to this day. But his ideas also made a special appeal to the peasantry in the south, for his hostility was levelled not so much at the landowners as against the state and therefore fitted the mentality of a population which had come to look upon the state as the symbol of oppression and class interests.

In 1874 Bakunin stirred up an anarchist revolt in Romagna which ended in disaster. So did a similar rising in Benevento, where the peasants sacked the town hall and burnt the tax registers. Both risings were put down with bloodshed and Bakunin lost prestige. Leadership of the workers' movement passed to the socialists in Milan, who set up a Lombard federation of the International. The movement was far from being united. It had a so-called democratic side which thought the workers should keep out of politics and confine their attention to wage claims and the like. Basically this part of the movement was ready to accept the paternalism which was already becoming a distinctive feature of Italian big industry. At the other extreme there was still a fair sprinkling of revolutionary anarchists ready to repeat the experiment of 1873. Andrea Costa, who had been a leader of that unhappy revolt, persuaded the socialists to follow the example of their French comrades and take part in elections with a view to achieving their aims through Parliament. To this end the Italian Socialist party was founded by Costa, Filippo Turati and others in 1892.

The party was born in Milan of a marriage between the apostles of Socialism and the more empirical workers' movement. This had given active help to the peasants during the rural strikes in Emilia and its members were inclined to be suspicious of the middle-class socialist intellectuals, but once the two movements fused, the workers were overawed and Italian socialism embarked on its doctrinaire course. From the outset it was divided between the moderate reformists, led by Turati, and the supporters of a maximum programme of social revolution as preached by the International. Both trends were influenced by the contemporary vogue of positivism and Darwinian theories of progress. The internationalists thought revolution was inevitable and the bourgeois state on the verge of collapse. The reformists believed that sooner or later parliamentary democracy must bring the proletariat to power. Antonio Labriola, Italy's first marxist philosopher, tried to combat this facile determinism without success.

The cleavage between the two trends, reformist and revolutionary, is a biological condition of Italian socialism. Expulsions, schisms and reunifications have characterized the movement from its beginnings to the present day. Relations with the trade-union movement[1] were never satisfactorily defined. The maximalists tended to think the party should dominate the unions, but this view was not shared by the syndicalists and led to much friction. Uneasy relations with the unions and an insoluble conflict between the philosophies of revolution and reform might have destroyed Italian socialism, instead of merely weakening it, had it not been for the astonishing vitality of the quasi-mystical belief in the unity of the working classes. Throughout all their vicissitudes Italian socialists have clung to this ideal as an article of faith and though it no longer commands the same blind devotion as in the past, its influence on socialist behaviour is still potent.

The Sicilian rising of 1893 soon put the Socialist Party to the test. This outbreak, known as the Fasci Siciliani,[2] shook Italian society deeply. One cause of unrest was a fall in the price of sulphur, which brought distress to 50,000 workers in the Sicilian sulphur mines. Misfortunes had been piling up since the introduction of the new tariffs in 1887. Following the example of northern Italy, some 300 peasant leagues or fasci had sprung in up Sicily. Membership was about 200,000 strong and the leaders, some of whom were socialists, hoped to teach the peasants the rudiments of discipline and organized action, but after a series of strikes the movement got out of hand. The women urged their menfolk to violence and the demonstrators attacked custom houses and tax offices, sacked the town halls and burned the registers. They threatened the landowners and squatted on the land. To all appearances it was a typical outburst of *jacquerie*. The rioters carried banners in honour of Marx, the Virgin and 'our good King Humbert' (as in Richard II's England, the peasants thought the monarch would defend them against the wicked barons).

This ideological naïveté shocked the socialist intellectuals in Milan and even the workers who, in northern Italy, were generally republican and anticlerical. Turati himself at first thought the peasants were following the same pattern as in the risings of 1799 and the 1860's –

38

distrust of the 'reactionary' peasantry was inherited by the socialists from Mazzini – but he soon changed his mind and with some difficulty persuaded the party to support the peasants as 'unenlightened but legitimate' fighters in the common cause.

The first to understand the real nature and significance of this upheaval was Giolitti, then in his first term of office as premier. Giolitti saw that social discontents needed to be taken seriously and not just ruthlessly put down, but this attitude was too advanced for his contemporaries, who wanted military action against the 'rebels'. Giolitti, unjustly discredited by the revolt and by the bank scandals, fell from office and his career was interrupted for nine years. Crispi, who succeeded him, at once declared martial law. The rising of 1893–4 ended like all the others in bloodshed and deportations and widened the gulf between the governing class and the population.

The social troubles of the nineties sparked off a reaction in favour of authoritarianism. The liberals began to think their form of government was too democratic for such turbulent times. Sidney Sonnino, an outstanding member of the Right, proposed reviving the principle, inherent in Charles Albert's Statute, that each single minister should be responsible directly to the King. King Humbert did not welcome the idea but Crispi was followed as prime minister by the right-wing di Rudini and afterwards by General Pelloux, whom the Court encouraged to be tough with the mob. A regime of special laws, courts martial and deportations was introduced. To fight this assault on liberty Turati persuaded the socialists, much against their principles, to join forces with the Republicans and the Radicals in a 'League for the Defence of Freedom'. Pelloux's arbitrary government brought unpopularity on the King and perhaps contributed to the tragedy of his death. King Humbert was assassinated by an anarchist on 29 July 1900. Ironically, this occurred shortly after Pelloux had been dismissed and constitutional government restored.

Although the world economic crisis was over by 1898 and conditions in Italy were improving, a sudden rise in wheat prices during the Spanish-American war led to bread riots in Milan. Like all social agitation in Italy, both before and after fascism, these riots were

tinged with revolutionary folklore and greatly frightened the bourgeoisie. But the conditions which make revolution possible have
never existed in Italy, whose economy is dependent on imports.
Whether they admitted it or not, Italian revolutionaries, with the
exception of Bakunin and Mussolini, have always been inhibited by
the knowledge that, were they to seize power, they could be squeezed
out within a few months by a blockade which would leave the
country without fuel for its industry or wheat to feed the population.[3] These truths were more felt than admitted by the socialists in
1898 and were by no means evident to the liberals, who feared that
social disorder would lower Italy's prestige among the powers. The
turn of the century was a dark hour for the liberals, many of whom
had begun to think that government by the élite was doomed. The
belief that the liberal governing class had lost its grip was shared by
the socialists and by the catholics, who now emerged from their long
political eclipse. Both these groups represented vast sections of the
population and each thought its chance to take over from the
liberals was at hand.

After 1870 Italian catholics tended to sort themselves out into
diehards, moderates and progressives. There were intransigents who
wanted not only to restore the temporal power but to bring back the
old regime and tried to do so by blowing on the disaffection of the
peasants. The events of 1893, however, showed that the peasants
were no longer looking back to an imagined happier feudal past but
forward to the time when their claims would be recognized by the
state. The Church sensed this change of attitude and Leo XIII's
famous encyclical *Rerum Novarum*, issued in 1891, established two
important points of catholic social doctrine: the right of the workers
(including the peasants) to organize themselves in trade unions,
albeit preferably in guilds or 'corporations' which should include
their employers; and the duty of the state to intervene to see that
justice was done in labour disputes. This last point was recognized by
the catholics before the socialists had made up their mind whether
state intervention was desirable or not.

The liberal catholics, who had been so deeply mortified by the
Church in the days of Cavour, gradually recovered influence as it

became increasingly necessary for the Papacy to accept a compromise with the state, but they still received very little encouragement from the Vatican and their entry into politics was tolerated after 1904 on the understanding that they would give their votes, either as electors or as deputies, in exchange for very concrete concessions on matters of special interest to the Church. They were to oppose divorce and encourage state subsidies to religious schools and charities.

The liberal catholics had to contend not only with the coldness of the Vatican but with the hostility of the Christian Democrats, a new movement which had grown up on the catholic left. After 1870 the liberal 'persecutions' generated a new wave of Counter-Reformation fervour in Italy, giving birth to the movement known as Catholic Action. This was inspired by the Syllabus of Errors and sought to prepare a lay apostolate for a catholic counter-offensive against liberalism. Its aim was to reconquer Italy for Christianity by defending catholic dogma and catholic morals (as well as the independence of the Pope) against the 'tyranny' of the liberal state. A central executive, the Opera dei Congressi, was set up in 1875. The movement had a strong territorial base in Venetia but its network spread over the whole of Italy with committees in every diocese and parish. Like the original Counter-Reformation it was deeply concerned with education. Catholic schools and catholic charities were the main cares of Catholic Action but the movement also sought to get a foothold in local government. *The non expedit* of 1874 (p. 17) referred only to parliamentary elections, not to local administration, and Catholic Action soon became a political force in the provinces. It was also a great formative influence in the lives of young catholics, particularly during the dark years of liberal and later fascist ostracism, and provided the social and moral background to the generation of catholics who founded the Christian Democratic movement in the nineties. Again in the 1930's Catholic Action was the nursery for another generation of catholic politicians, the men who govern Italy today.

The Christian Democrats of the 1890's took their cue from the *Rerum Novarum*. They were socially progressive but politically antiliberal, not because they wanted to see the Pope's temporal power restored, but because they believed that the liberal state was the enemy of the working classes. They thought the liberals, after destroying feudal institutions, had left the masses isolated and defenceless against the forces of capitalism. They believed at first that catholics should abstain from liberal politics in order to cultivate and strengthen their own political and social creed. They were as hostile to the liberal catholics as to other liberals but their influence was curtailed by Pius X, who hated modernism and would not allow the Christian Democrats to form a party of their own.[4]

Liberal government, which had looked so shaky during the turbulent nineties, was to enjoy a period of respite thanks to the return of economic prosperity and the advent of a statesman of uncommon acumen and originality. From 1901 to 1914 Giovanni Giolitti's influence was paramount. During those years, except for a brief recession in 1907, and again during the Libyan war of 1912, the economy was expanding; Italy had a balanced budget and its international credit stood higher than at any time since unification. Social unrest was still endemic but so long as Giolitti was in office there was no question of resorting to extra-constitutional methods of repression. The nineteenth-century liberal system of government appeared to have reached its acme.

But Giolitti himself was aware that these were years of transition and that many characteristics of the society it befell him to govern were changing radically. It was his policy to allow these changes to take place as gently as possible so that no violent upheaval should wrest power from the hands of the small liberal governing class. Like the 'Leopard' in Lampedusa's novel, he knew that a great deal must change if things were to stay as they were. Success eluded him in the end partly because he failed to communicate his own reading of the situation to his contemporaries, but also because he overestimated his own capacity to dominate the forces of change. To many liberals as well as radicals his brilliant strategy appeared cynical and 'empirical', a term which, to Italians, is almost synonymous with 'unprincipled'. In reality, though Giolitti leaned politically to the Left it was in order to keep his boat in equilibrium. In style and character, in his preference for home affairs and good finance to foreign policy, he belonged to the best tradition of the old Italian Right. He was in fact a disciple of Quintino Sella.

When Giolitti took over, Italy was still on the threshold of industrial capitalism. The banks controlled industry, and development was largely dependent on foreign capital. In Parliament limited suffrage and single-member constituencies made politics a matter of personal relations between ministers, prefects, individual deputies and grand electors.[5] When he left office on the eve of World War I, industry was already tending to concentrate in cartels and industrial capital was more powerful than the banks. Italy was exporting capital to Turkey, North Africa and the Balkans. In Parliament the introduction of universal manhood suffrage (first applied in 1913) gave new importance to the rural constituencies and in the country the small liberal élite was being crowded out by the advent of new mass groups, socialist, nationalist and catholic. Roughly these represented respectively the industrial workers and the labourers of north-central Italy, the poor but educated middle class, and the peasantry. Giolitti's aim was to play off the catholics against the socialists in order to strengthen the position of the liberals and make the government a mediating power between the new social forces.

He was impressed by the captains of industry and approved their productivist philosophy but he was determined to make use of the fact that they had much to ask of government. In return for tariffs and other government favours he pressed employers to raise wages and generally improve the conditions of the workers, for his ultimate purpose was to create a breach between the privileged industrial workers and the rest of the proletariat and to translate this into political terms by dividing the socialist reformists from the maximalists in the hope of splitting the Socialist party. To this end he would not allow the police, still less the army, to interfere in wage strikes as Crispi and Pelloux had done. Government neutrality in wage disputes strengthened the hands of the reformists and Giolitti's 'system' was based on a tacit understanding with the reformist leader Turati who, like himself, was a pragmatist. But Giolitti never succeeded in his grand design of enticing Turati into government and so definitely splitting the Socialist party.

43

The weakness of Giolitti's system was the narrowness of its social basis. The alliance between big industry and a working-class 'aristocracy' left a large area of the population dissatisfied. His enemies accused him of promoting a plutocracy. In reality he believed that the progress of the working classes was inevitable and the first duty of an enlightened democracy was to abolish ignorance, superstition, and illiteracy. He repeatedly tried to introduce a progressive income-tax and though he knew that this measure would be thrown out by Parliament in 1905, there is no reason to doubt that he sincerely believed it would be beneficial. Had the liberals accepted his reform he would not have needed to fall back on the indirect taxes which made the poorer strata of the population pay for the public works, the wage increases and the welfare laws which improved the lot of the workers in northern Italy. This policy, coupled with the questionable methods he used to put his own men into Parliament in the southern constituencies, brought upon him the wrath of the radical *meridionalisti*[6] but in fact Giolitti was the first Italian statesman to favour state intervention in the economy with a view to helping the south.

Giolitti's social and economic policies were ahead of his times but his political methods were the quintessence of nineteenth-century *trasformismo*. His problem was to govern the country through Parliament without a party of his own, at a time when organized, ideologically coherent parties were taking shape. His own majority was hand-picked and personally loyal but it was never a living organism. The socialists were the first political party to emerge and, with the country in a state of chronic social agitation, they naturally dominated Giolitti's horizon, but he soon perceived that the catholics, with an equally powerful dogma and all the apparatus of organization ready to hand, could become a formidable political quantity. He approached them in the same way as the socialists, that is by trying to divide the moderates from the doctrinaire fanatics. The task was made easy at first by the tacit co-operation of the Vatican which, like himself, had no desire to see the birth of a zealous Counter-Reformation party. But there was a third group, the nationalists, forerunners of the future fascist movement, whom

44

Giolitti underrated from the start, partly perhaps because their ideology was so completely alien to his own way of thought. He considered nationalism a caricature of patriotism and dangerous to liberal government.

Two trends of quite different origin combined to produce the peculiar blend of nationalism that was to lead Italy on to fascism. There was the old-fashioned nostalgic irredentism inherited from the Risorgimento, and the newfangled nationalistic philosophy of violence elaborated by the leaders of *Action Française* and imported into Italy from France. The idea that Trentino and Trieste must be 'redeemed' before Italy could be nationally fulfilled was originally a left-wing aspiration fostered by Mazzini and Garibaldi, but when the socialists ousted the republicans as the dominant element in the Left, irredentism lost its appeal for men who thought a new international order was at hand. It was taken up by the Right and became the romantic and respectable cover for Italy's economic and financial thrust towards the Balkans. The upsurge of strong Italian feeling in the 'unredeemed' territories after 1860 is easy to understand and the socialists showed characteristic lack of realism in refusing to take it into account. Before Venetia passed to Italy the Italians in the Austrian Empire had been a strong and privileged minority of five million with access to careers in the services and the administration. After 1866 they became a distrusted minority of 800,000, debarred from public service and struggling to survive against Germans, Magyars and Southern Slavs. The introduction of manhood suffrage in the Austrian Empire in 1907 was a direct threat to the Italian population in the towns, and irredentism spread from Trieste to the whole of Istria and the Dalmatian coast. It focussed emotionally on the Adriatic, D'Annunzio's 'Bitter Sea'. In 1908 D'Annunzio published his turgid play, *The Ship*, which sang the glory of the old Venetian Republic, and soon the irredentists were coveting all that had ever belonged to Venice.

Another stimulus to Italian nationalism occurred in 1908 when Austria formally annexed the Turkish province of Bosnia–Hercegovina without consulting the powers. There was no question of compensation to Italy, who expected it in virtue of the Triple

45

Alliance and of the doctrine invented by Cesare Balbo[7] that Austria should make room for Italy by moving east. Instead the Austrians added insult to injury by refusing to open a university for Italian students at Trento. Italy was on the verge of war with Austria in 1908 (the Austrians thought of attacking while the Italian army was helping to clear the wreckage from the earthquake at Messina) and henceforth irredentism and nationalism joined hands. Thanks largely to the personal inclination of King Victor Emmanuel III, irredentism had penetrated the Court and military circles while nationalism, on the flamboyant French model, was fashionable among intellectuals and encouraged by newspaper-owning business interests engaged in the Balkan and Turkish trade. In 1910 the writer Enrico Corradini founded the Nationalist Movement and propounded the doctrine that Italy was a proletarian nation struggling for a place in the sun.

Corradini had been sincerely shocked at the plight of Italian emigrants in North and South America. During the first decade of the century emigration was running at the rate of 600,000 a year, rising to a peak of 873,000 in 1913. To classically educated Italians it was a shock to find that in the new world their nation was despised as illiterate and underdeveloped. But whereas Giolitti and, at first, even Mussolini thought the answer was to build schools and public works in the south, the nationalists concluded that Italy should have colonies of its own where its emigrants would be treated with respect. The picture of poor Italian emigrants struggling for exist-ence overseas was matched, in nationalist ideology, by a similar image of Italian capital struggling to get a foothold in foreign markets where it had been preceded by the British, Germans and French. The old obsession that Italy would not be in time to get a share of the Turkish tart was translated into the new concept of Italy as a 'proletarian nation'.

By 1910 Giolitti's carefully balanced system of government was in danger of being upset by the new trends which had developed on Left and Right. The disorganized but genuine aspiration of the masses to a place inside the democratic system was matched by an equally powerful and more aggressive swing towards nationalism

46

within the governing class. Numerically the nationalist movement represented a minority on the liberal Right but there were powerful financial interests behind it and its propaganda made a wide appeal to the poor but educated middle classes, the students and teachers and state employees who formed Italy's newspaper-reading public. Two generations reared on the patriotic verse of Carducci and the patriotic music of Verdi were easily beguiled by the new nationalist message. Giolitti had no esteem for public opinion – he thought it prone to extremism and never satisfied – but he feared it even though he was generally more sensitive to feeling in Parliament than in the country. In a desperate effort to save the system of rational government he had so brilliantly revived, he conceived the idea of appeasing Left and Right simultaneously by introducing universal suffrage to please the Left and seizing the Turkish province of Libya to please the Right.

Giolitti planned his Libyan war as coolly as Cavour had planned his intervention in the Crimea. It was a purely political move. He had no enthusiasm for colonial adventures but he thought that a short colonial war would satisfy the Right and that no liberal government could survive should Italy lose this last chance of seizing a colony in North Africa. The timing was conditioned by the French attack on Morocco, for the two African territories were linked by international diplomacy and once France had consolidated her protectorate over Morocco she would have no interest in allowing Italy to grab Libya.

The war began in September 1911 and ended with the cession of Libya to Italy at the Treaty of Ouchy in October 1912. It was not a military triumph for the Italians. In April 1912 Italy occupied Rhodes and the Dodecanese islands in the Aegean, to which she held on after the war – she was to lose them to Greece in 1947 – but the Turks gave in finally only because war had broken out in the Balkans. (Italy's Libyan war sparked off a series of upheavals that were to lead to Sarajevo.) As for the colony, it was pacified with great difficulty and the Italians were not in full control there until 1931. At immense cost they reclaimed parts of the country from the desert, and large-scale settlement of Cyrenaica began in 1935. Seven years later the Italians had to abandon the colony and the desert has since crept over many of their farms.

In 1912 Parliament accepted Giolitti's argument that men who can fight for their country have the right to vote and in 1913 Italians returned their first Parliament elected by universal male suffrage. The widening of the suffrage meant that government could no longer manage elections in the old way without resorting to wide-scale violence. Giolitti did not shrink from this but even so the structure of the new Parliament was different from the Chambers he had managed for so long. The liberals dropped from 382 to 310 but 228 liberal deputies owed their seats to the catholic vote. The extreme Left rose from 110 to 169 and one-third of the deputies entered the Chamber for the first time. This raw and inexperienced assembly was to be caught in the hurricane of World War I.

1, 2 Founding fathers of united Italy: Mazzini (*above, left*), whose
'Young Italy' movement spearheaded the struggle for independence;
Cavour (*above, right*), liberal and anticlerical, first prime minister of the
new kingdom.

3 On 11 May 1860 Garibaldi landed at Marsala, Sicily (*below*), with a
thousand red-shirted volunteers. The 'March of the Thousand' rode the
crest of a peasants' uprising, briefly transforming it into a patriotic war
to drive out the Bourbons and unite Italy under King Victor Emmanuel
II (though many of the Thousand, and even Garibaldi himself, would
have preferred a republic).

4–6 The first decades of independence brought little but poverty and oppression to the south. In the Sicilian sulphur mines (*above*), where the incidence of TB was almost 100 per cent, children worked long hours. Naples (*left*) became, as it largely still is, a town of squalid, crowded tenements. For many thousands, emigration was the only solution. Between 1900 and 1913 emigration averaged 626,000 a year, nearly half of which came from the south. The family on the right were photographed in 1905 on Ellis Island, the quarantine station in New York harbour.

7 King Victor Emmanuel III at the front in 1915. Puny and unimpressive though he was, he had the typical militaristic fervour of the House of Savoy.

8 Arditi, former 'commando'-type fighters of World War I. The fascists appropriated their black shirts and their glamour to capture the imagination of Italian youth.

9 The making of a myth: the 'march on Rome', 1922. Mussolini (in
sash) travelled down by train the next day. Before leaving Milan he
required a cable from the King offering him the premiership.

10 Cardinal Gasparri and Mussolini signing the Lateran Pacts on 11
February 1929. From now on, the Pope was recognized as sovereign of
an independent state, the Vatican City.

11 Under the stress of trying to keep up with his more powerful ally
Hitler (*above*), Mussolini began to show signs of instability even before
the so-called 'Pact of Steel' dragged Italy into Hitler's war.

12 The Ospedale Maggiore, Milan, built by Francesco Sforza in the
fifteenth century, was bombed and badly damaged in 1943.

13 After Mussolini's overthrow, Italian troops fought on the Allied side, their status the new one of 'co-belligerents'. On the British Eighth Army front, the Archbishop of Catanzara celebrates mass in the field; the Italian royalist flag is displayed behind the altar.

14 In April 1945, partisan forces drove the Germans out of Milan. After the battle, partisan leaders addressed the crowd (*right*). Standing on the roof of a car, his arms folded, is Luigi Longo, Spanish Civil War veteran, leader of the communist partisans, and now, since the death of Togliatti, leader of the Italian Communist Party.

15 Four statesmen representing the antifascist parties who have played a leading part in rebuilding Italy. From left to right: Ivanoe Bonomi, Pietro Nenni, Alcide de Gasperi, Giuseppe Saragat.

16, 17 *Below, left*: Enrico Mattei talking to workers of ENI. His exploitation of Italy's natural gas and his battle with private oil interests were a determining factor in the 'Italian miracle' of the 1950's. *Below, right*: Palmiro Togliatti, leader of the Italian Communist Party until his death in 1964, and, to the Russians, one of the most respected Communist leaders of the west.

4   War and peace

BETWEEN 1912 AND 1914 Giolitti's carefully poised system broke
down. The Libyan war and universal suffrage hastened its end.
Instead of placating the nationalists, as Giolitti apparently hoped, the
war encouraged them and enhanced their prestige while it acted as a
challenge and a stimulus to the Left. In this upheaval the reformists
lost the leadership of the Socialist party to the maximalists, among
whom Mussolini now came to the fore. Both factions opposed the
Libyan war on principle because it was waged by a bourgeois state,
but on the party's extreme right Bissolati and a few others, whose
ideology was more radical than socialist, supported a colonial war
which Mazzini himself might have approved. They were expelled in
1912 and formed an independent reformist socialist party whose
only influence derived from Bissolati's personal prestige. As this was
considerable his defection weakened the socialist front. Turati
remained unhappily with the main party where the reformists
never recovered control. The Libyan war had the support of a
good many syndicalists, particularly southerners who seem to have
believed that Libya could provided land for two million Italian
peasants. Many of them were persuaded by Labriola's theory that
war would prepare the nation for revolution.[1] Mussolini was to
adopt this view in November 1914 but in 1911 he violently and
dogmatically opposed the Libyan war. These conflicts lacerated the
Italian Left and foreshadowed the far more dramatic dispute
between neutralists and interventionists that was to divide the
country on the outbreak of World War I.

Turati's eclipse meant that Giolitti could no longer count on
socialist support which had been the essence of his system. He
turned of necessity to the moderate catholics whose demands for

the Church dismayed the old anticlerical liberals. This narrow, self-complacent élite was no longer strong enough to govern Italy yet the illusion that the liberals could hang on to their traditional monopoly of power caused many of them to favour Italy's intervention in the Great War. They thought that mobilization would keep the socialists and catholics in check while victory would strengthen the old governing class.

Giolitti imagined that his personal influence was still intact. He controlled over three hundred deputies and every prefect and high official in the country owed him his place, but outside Parliament the old man was isolated and unpopular. His unexpansive temperament and dry, precise style, which is admired today, unfitted him to please a generation fired by nationalist rodomontade. Among the intellectuals the fashion had turned against positivism and nine-teenth-century enlightenment. The literary world was dominated by D'Annunzio's gory decadentism, the arts by Marinetti's futurist[2] absurdities and the philosophers were engrossed in an elaborate revival of idealism. They despised Giolitti as the incarnation of prosaic rationalism. The entire intelligentsia, with the exception of Croce, was against him, and even Croce did more, unintentionally, to destroy than to save the system he admired. He had come to look down on science and was digging a grave for positivism in which Italians were to bury common sense.

The Libyan war and its aftermath brought economic distress and sparked off a period of social unrest culminating in the 'red week' of June 1914. For a while it seemed that revolutionary socialism had got the upper hand in east-central Italy. In Emilia, Romagna and the Marches there were enclaves of socialist power amounting almost to miniature republics. Local government was in their hands, and their leagues and co-operatives and their Labour Chambers were strong enough to make the farmers accept their terms. At Ancona, in June 1914, the socialists actually proclaimed a republic and held out against regular troops for a week. The landowners, despairing of help from government so long as Giolitti was in power, raised armed bands to harry the socialists and break the incessant rural strikes. Recourse to a private militia is recurrent in Italian history.

No language has more words to describe such bands. Those operating against the socialists in 1913–14 were precursors of the fascist squads that were to appear in central Italy after the war.

It was during these battles that Mussolini became a hero to the socialists of his home region, the Romagna. They began to call him Duce, the title that had been Garibaldi's. In 1912 Mussolini became editor of the party paper *Avanti*. His declared aim was to prepare the proletariat psychologically for the use of violence. He was in search of a platform, and behind his vehemently expressed opinions he had no firm ideological conviction and would embrace whatever current theory seemed most likely to favour his plans. Sorel, Bergson and Pareto may have influenced his thinking, as Croce supposed, but their ideas served to provide him with arms for his personal battle. The cult of violence, the exaltation of action and will, the doctrine of government by the élite were part of his equipment. Below the surface he was a product of the rural anarchist tradition Bakunin had planted in the Romagna. He never understood the facts of industrial economy and for a socialist he was not well grounded in Marx. Conflict with the party's doctrinaire leaders was inevitable, for Mussolini was too ambitious and too impatient to wait for the socialist millennium. The controversy over intervention gave him the opportunity to break with the party from a position of strength.

As the socialists swung over to maximalism on the eve of the first World War, the middle classes in Italy, as in Europe, veered sharply to the Right. In May 1914 the nationalists moved out of the liberal fold to form a party of their own with the backing of heavy industry and high finance. The liberals themselves were moving towards irredentism and expansionism under the guidance of their press. Newspapers such as *Il Corriere della Sera, Il Messaggero* and others had acquired great influence and prestige, and their editors played an important part in bringing Italy into the war.

In March 1914 Giolitti, defeated on a tax bill, handed over the premiership to the right-wing liberal, Antonio Salandra. This was to have been another of Giolitti's strategic retreats but he was caught out of office when the war started in August and it took him six years to get back. He was passionately convinced that Italy should stay neutral. He had renewed the Triple Alliance on the eve of his own Libyan war and he believed the spirit, if not the letter, of the Alliance required Italy to be friendly to the Central Powers. He had already come to regret the Libyan adventure and saw no advantage to be gained by war that could not be got by diplomacy. He knew Italy was not prepared for a European conflict and thought nothing could prevent the Austrians from reaching Milan, but his famous phrase that 'much' could have been obtained from Austria by negotiation was never supported by any concrete suggestion about terms. Giolitti was in a dilemma. He wanted Italy to be neutral because he thought she was weak. At the same time he wanted to sell her neutrality to Austria for the highest price he could get. He knew that his own position in favour of neutrality made the Austrians hold back and he dared not form a neutralist government (for which he could have found a majority in Parliament) lest this should make Austria refuse even a slice of the Trentino. His behaviour was therefore ambiguous and his opponents thought he was playing safe in the hope of returning to office later with unsoiled hands, an idea he most certainly caressed. Salandra and his foreign minister, Sonnino, Giolitti's old rival, were determined to prevent this at all costs. They feared that Giolitti's return would strengthen the socialists and catholics – for different reasons both groups were in favour of neutrality – and cause the old-fashioned liberals to be swamped. This was an inevitable consequence of the extension of the suffrage but its effects were delayed for a while by the war. Home politics played an important part in deciding the government for intervention.

The story of Italy's entry into World War I shows how a determined group of individuals can use a vociferous minority to carry their point against the wishes of the majority. The same tactics were to succeed in October 1922. Salandra himself admitted that Italy's intervention was conceived and desired by an active but very small minority which the government could easily have restrained.

When hostilities started in August 1914 Italy declared neutrality and began at once to negotiate with both sides. This was normal diplomatic practice. Germany and Austria had not consulted her. The Triple Alliance did not oblige her to support an aggressive war and explicitly excluded hostilities against Britain. Italy had territorial claims against Austria and expansionist ambitions in the Balkans. From a diplomatic viewpoint she could sell either her neutrality to Austria or her participation to the Entente. It was logical to find out which side offered more. But at a very early stage King Victor Emmanuel, Salandra and Sonnino became eager for intervention against Austria for this was in the tradition of the Risorgimento and the House of Savoy. All three were deeply concerned to strengthen the monarchy, which seemed threatened by the revival of militant republicanism among the socialists. Even among the interventionists there were figures like D'Annunzio and Mussolini who openly inclined towards a republic, and there was a danger that monarchists might shift their loyalty from the puny and unimpressive sovereign to his more soldierly cousins of the Aosta branch. To the King and his ministers, in the winter of 1914–15, it looked as though nothing but the satisfaction through victory of Italy's territorial claims could make the country safe for the dynasty and the old liberal élite.

Sonnino knew as well as Salandra that the majority of Italians were not in favour of war but, like his colleague, he believed that war and peace were matters for the King and his ministers to decide 'above the heads of the crowd'. The motives of these three men were ennobled by reminiscences of the Risorgimento – throughout the hostilities King Victor Emmanuel was constantly at the front – and they certainly believed in the doctrine of 'sacred egoism' which Salandra announced to explain the change of alliance in May 1915. But theirs were not the motives for which the democratic interventionists were pressing the government to declare war and for which so many Italians were to lay down their lives in the belief that they were fighting for the freedom of nations and the rights of man.

From the outset Italy's democratic Left was eager to fight with France. Cesare Battisti[3] and the irredentists of Trentino and Trieste and dissident socialists like Salvemini and Bissolati were among the first to call for intervention on the side of France, and by December 1914 some 4,000 Italian volunteers were fighting with the French

Foreign Legion in the Argonne. The revolutionary syndicalists, led by Filippo Corridoni and Michele Bianchi, were also for helping the French and set up interventionist Fasci for revolutionary action. Mussolini was to join forces with them after his breach with the socialists. The nationalists, who were a right-wing party that had peeled off from the liberals, were uncertain at first on which side Italy should fight. They were for war at any price and some preferred Germany to France. There was much admiration for German discipline and culture among Italian conservatives. But the logic of Italy's territorial claims against Austria soon caused the nationalists to make common cause with the democratic and revolutionary interventionists who were clamouring for Italy to side with the Triple Entente. Last but not least, liberal newspapers like *Il Corriere della Sera* embraced the cause of intervention against Austria.

Mussolini had realized from the start that the war would break up the Socialist International and hoped to see the Italian Socialist party side with France. For a few weeks he toed the party line of rigid neutrality but in September 1914 he was intriguing with the nationalists, and on 18 October he announced in *Avanti* a complete change of heart 'from absolute to active neutrality'. He left the editorship and was expelled from the Socialist party on 24 November but in the meanwhile, with help from the conservative nationalist paper *Il Resto del Carlino* and a probable secret subvention from the French government, he had started his own paper, *Il Popolo d'Italia*, which became the main organ of the interventionist Left. For the rest of his career Mussolini was to be financed and supported by the Right but to speak, and perhaps even believe that he was acting, in the name of the proletariat.

The advocates of neutrality far outnumbered the interventionists but they too were a mixed lot. In Parliament some three hundred deputies were for keeping Italy out of the war and would have stood by Giolitti had he given them a lead. In the country the socialists were the most articulate opponents of intervention and in northern Italy there were violent clashes between the two sides. But the catholics were also unenthusiastic about the war. They had supported the Libyan adventure with some encouragement from the Vatican, whose financial interests were involved, but in 1914 the Vatican cherished Austria as the only loyal first-class catholic power and saw nothing to be gained for the Church from the victory of the Entente. Vatican diplomacy took a hand in the negotiations with Austria with a view to keeping Italy out of the war or, if the worst came to the worst, to securing a place for the Vatican at the peace conference. It would, however, be a misreading of Benedict XV's pontificate to see nothing but ecclesiastical politics behind the pacifism of this remarkable Pope. Giacomo della Chiesa was the forerunner of John XXIII, and his celebrated phrase 'stop this useless slaughter', uttered in 1917, came from the heart. It was misconstrued in Italy by the government and the generals as an attempt to undermine the country's morale.

The mass of Italian peasants was unmoved by the controversy over intervention but naturally preferred peace to war. The peasants were mobilized and sent to the front with the promise that when they came home they would be given land of their own.

On 26 April 1915 Italy signed the Treaty of London with Britain, France and Russia, pledging herself to enter the war on the side of the Allies within a month. The treaty guaranteed that after victory her eastern frontier would be moved to the Brenner and along the Julian Alps. She was to receive Istria, central Dalmatia (not Fiume) and Valona, which she had already seized, and the Allies would help her to round off her colonies after the war. The Treaty handed over to Italy some 230,000 Germans and some 700,000 Slavs and thus ignored the principle of nationalities. The Italian negotiators were thinking entirely in terms of security and the balance of power. Their aim was to give Italy strong frontiers and absolute control of the Adriatic. Salandra and Sonnino imagined that once these aims had been achieved the Austro-Hungarian Empire, shorn of Trentino, Trieste and Dalmatia, could resist the claims of its other subject peoples and form a defensive alliance with Italy against the Slavs. The last thing these old-fashioned liberals desired was to destroy the European 'concert of nations' which, like Cavour, they identified with civilization. They quite failed to appreciate the strength of Slav nationalism or the importance to Italy of friendly relations with the

Serbs. By staking a claim to Dalmatia they played into the hands of the Italian nationalists and put the country onto the road that was to lead to Fiume and thence to fascism. It was not until 1917 that Italians learned the text of this treaty – divulged by the Bolsheviks – which was to cause such bitter controversy after the war.

Up to the last the Austrians did not really expect Italy to enter the war against them. They overestimated the influence of Giolitti and the neutralists and put too much confidence in the Pope. The concessions they offered were tardy and insufficient and were probably not made in good faith. Unlike the Italian ministers, the Austrian government was always acutely aware that it could cede nothing on the empire's western frontier without producing a landslide on the east.

With the Treaty of London signed, Salandra had four weeks in which to prepare the nation and Parliament for war. He turned to D'Annunzio to orchestrate Italy's 'Radiant May'. D'Annunzio laid on one of the first great political public-relations stunts in the history of modern times. In Rome the demonstrations spilled over from the piazza into Parliament. The deputies were scared. Giolitti had deserted them and on 20 May they voted the government full power for war by 407 to 74. The neutralist majority had completely vanished and only Turati spoke against. Mussolini and the nationalists rejoiced that Parliament – Italy's 'bubonic plague' – had been humiliated but Turati noted sadly that the first effect of war had been to destroy the vigour and dignity of parliamentary institutions.

The Socialists reacted faintly. There was a strike in Milan with barricades but it was easily overcome, and the general strike called on 19 May was a flop. Socialist morale was undermined by the spectacle of the German and French socialist parties each supporting the national war effort. The Second International had virtually collapsed. The Italian Socialist party still clung to its official pacifism but its slogan during the war was 'neither support nor sabotage'.

With a lightness of heart unforgivable in men who claimed to be acting on rational calculation, Salandra, Sonnino and the King plunged Italy into a war whose cost and dimension they had never paused to reckon. Their great fear had been that the war might end before Italy had chosen its partners, and in the negotiations for the Treaty of London they failed to insist on adequate financial aid or supplies of coal (still being imported from Germany), munitions and raw materials. Italy, whose consumption of steel and coal per head was greatly inferior to Austria's, had neither the industrial capacity nor the financial strength necessary to hold out against more highly developed capitalist countries. In fact the Austrians had assumed that for this reason, if for no other, the Italians would not pit themselves against the Central Powers. The only thing Italy had in full supply was manpower, but the government had not foreseen that with full-scale mobilization the country would need more food than it had consumed in peacetime.

A country that is relieved to see half a million citizens emigrate yearly is not likely to be fussy about sending tens of thousands of troops into battle against fearful odds. The Italian commander-in-chief, Luigi Cadorna, was a stiff-necked Piedmontese general whose approach to the war was conditioned by the fact that men were plentiful and weapons scarce. He was also influenced by the prevailing mood in Italy that every inch of ground gained from the enemy was sacred, however difficult and costly to hold. Again and again he sent the infantry into attack against machine-gun barrages without cover from the artillery. The officers were armed with swords. The soldiers were told to cut the barbed-wire entanglements with garden secateurs and, if these were lacking, to *use their teeth*. The Italians were fighting uphill on a four-hundred-mile front in difficult mountainous country, and though they outnumbered the Austrians by almost four to one they were short of artillery and munitions and their losses were tragic. After thirty years of military alliance with Austria the Italian command had no defence works or plans for operations on the eastern front, yet Cadorna was determined to prove that Napoleon was wrong when he asserted that it was hopeless to attack Austria from the Isonzo river unless one held the Trentino region, further north. In two years the Italians fought eleven battles on the Isonzo, advancing twenty-five miles towards Trieste with a loss of 200,000 men.

None of the belligerents in World War I were tender with their troops but the Italian Command was unique in its disregard of human factors. Cadorna was obsessed by the pacifist murmurs from the home front. He thought that troops must be flogged into battle, if necessary by firing on them from the rear. When his plans went wrong he would dismiss his generals and have the soldiers shot, and he told the government he would resort, if necessary, to decimation. For the men at the front there were no periods of rest behind the lines and home leave was extremely rare. Since there were deserters in Sicily special orders were given that Sicilians were never to be sent home. Two years of this treatment unnerved the career officers and almost broke the Army's morale. None the less, in the summer of 1917, it gathered strength for a heroic advance onto the Bainsizza plateau on the promise that this was the last great effort needed to end the war. When the army discovered that nothing permanent had been gained by its sacrifice, it lost heart.

The collapse of Russia enabled the Austrians to concentrate their entire army on the Italian front in October 1917. With the help of seven picked German divisions they broke through the Italian lines at Caporetto and forced the Italians to retreat. The order to withdraw threw the Italian army into confusion. Psychologically and militarily it was geared only for attack. As the Italians withdrew from the Isonzo to the Tagliamento and thence to the Piave the retreat became a rout and the troops found the roads jammed by 400,000 civilian refugees. Italian losses at Caporetto were 10,000 killed, 30,000 wounded and 300,000 prisoners. Another 300,000 soldiers reached the Piave without arms.

Caporetto was not more disastrous than other reverses suffered by the Allies in World War I. Under a new command the Italians soon rallied and a year later, with the help of three British and two French divisions, they turned the tables on the Austrians – and ended their war – at Vittorio Veneto. But psychologically Caporetto is a landmark in Italian history. Cadorna himself dramatized the defeat in his famous communiqué accusing the Second Army of cowardice. He alleged that the Army's morale was sapped by pacifist propaganda from the socialists and from the Pope.

Fifty years after the event historians see the main cause of defeat in the lack of clarity and agreement over strategic plans and in Cadorna's disbelief in the coming attack. He was convinced the Austrians would not move before the spring. But the disorderly retreat was a premonitory sign of the great social upheaval that was to erupt in Italy after the war. Contemporaries thought that the socialists had corrupted the army and looked on Caporetto as a military strike. They saw that an army of recently enfranchised peasants was revolting against a despotic military élite and took this for the first rumbling of revolution. Only a more discerning observer like Angelo Gatti (Cadorna's staff officer and military historian) noticed that the malaise started in the Army and was affecting the country rather than the reverse. But he too foresaw the outcome in the form of a socialist revolution. Wise after the event, historians now see that Caporetto was not only the moment of truth for the peasant soldiers and the career officers of the high command, it was also a drama for the draft officers who were blamed for the disaster caused by the incompetence of the military chiefs. For these men Caporetto and its aftermath of disputes and ill-feeling was the beginning of a persecution that was to continue after the war, adding to the sense of grievance of the middle class to which they belonged. Demobilized and humiliated after 1918, these men were to turn to fascism for their redemption in 1921–22.

Italy lost 600,000 men in World War I and had to find pensions for over a million disabled. The money cost of the war was reckoned at 148,000 million lire, more than twice as much as her governments had spent in the half-century of national unity. Considering the country's resources, Italy's war effort was perhaps even greater than that of her allies. Certainly the war put an immense strain on a population which was used to individual hardship but had not yet been called on to make a collective sacrifice. After Caporetto the country made a supreme attempt, unique in its history, to stand united. Doctrinaire socialists like Turati and Treves stopped their anti-war talk and only the maximalists, under Serrati, remained intransigent in their hostility to the war. But when tension relaxed after victory and Italians had to face the difficulties and disappointments of peacemaking, their ideological disputes broke out afresh. The country was still divided between those who had wanted Italy to fight and those who had not, but an equally bitter and substantially more fatal conflict divided the democratic interventionists from the nationalists. Before the United States entered the war these two groups had been able to overlook the fact that they were fighting for different ends, but when President Wilson called on the Allies to define their war aims, concealment became impossible for the issue turned on Italy's relations with its future neighbour Yugoslavia.

The nationalists insisted on claiming all and more than had been promised to Italy in the Treaty of London: Istria, a large part of Dalmatia and a foothold in the Balkans, plus Smyrna which the Allies had assigned to Italy in the Treaty of St Jean de Maurienne. Against these maximum claims the democratic interventionists, whose spokesmen were Salvemini and the social-democratic minister Bissolati, were content to abide by the principle of nationalities, which they had proclaimed long before Wilson made it his own. This group had always held that the Austrian empire must be broken up into its component nations and that Italy should cultivate the friendship of all the successor states. Bissolati in particular saw clearly that unless Italy gave these new countries the kind of political and cultural leadership they were seeking, France would do so, perhaps to Italy's disadvantage.

Early in 1918 Italy had the chance to lay the foundation for a sound policy of friendship with nascent Yugoslavia. At the time Britain and France were willing to negotiate a separate peace with Austria which would have damaged the position of the subject nationalities, including the Italians of Istria and Trentino. President Wilson had already announced his famous fourteen points, one of which declared that peoples should no longer be bartered about like chattels from one sovereignty to another. In the name of President Wilson's newly defined principle of self-determination the Italian democrats organized a congress of the Oppressed Peoples of the Habsburg Empire which met in Rome in April 1918. The delegates

68

signed a pact in which Italians and Yugoslavs agreed to solve their frontier problems in such a way as not to hurt the vital interests of either country and resolved to observe the principle of nationalities. The pact clearly echoed President Wilson's admonition that Italy's eastern frontier must be readjusted 'along clearly recognized lines of nationality'. In that tense spring, when Italy was gathering strength for her last offensive against Austria, no one faced up to the fact that 'clearly recognized lines of nationality' simply did not exist on the eastern side of the Adriatic seaboard.

The so-called 'Pact of Rome' was not an official document though it seems to have been sponsored by the prime minister, Orlando. It was welcomed not only by the democratic interventionists but by the nationalists (including eccentrics like D'Annunzio and Mussolini) and by the generals, who hoped the good will shown to the Slavs would induce the Serb and Croat regiments in the Austrian army to mutiny. But the Serbs and Croats, who had made themselves hated in Italy during the Risorgimento, fought bitterly on the Italian front to the end of the war and so helped to dissipate the ephemeral good will created by the Pact of Rome.

The Italians signed their armistice with Austria on 4 November 1918 and proceeded to occupy the territories promised to Italy by the Treaty of London. These did not include Fiume, which remained under joint Allied occupation. But in 1918 even democrats like Salvemini thought the town should belong to Italy since its population was predominantly Italian. The nationalists also claimed Fiume. Their party was supported by business interests which feared that, in Yugoslav hands, the port would draw the Balkan trade away from Trieste.

At the Peace Conference Italy's allies made little demur about leaving her Trieste and a strategic frontier running from the Brenner to the Monte Nevoso but the Istrian and Dalmatian territories promised in the Treaty of London became subjects of contention. Britain and France, no less than the United States, had conceived a special tenderness for Yugoslavia which made them unwilling to honour the promises they had made in 1915. When those promises were made Britain and France were seeking to limit the expansion of Russian influence towards the Mediterranean. They preferred Italy to have the Dalmatian cities rather than see them go to Serbia, the protégé of Czarist Russia and the possible bridge-head for a Russian drive to the 'warm waters'. In 1918 this objective had ceased to exist. Russia was in the throes of revolution and had ceased to worry the Allies as a great power. Serbia had disappeared into the wider, but not very powerful, kingdom of Yugoslavia. Hence the lack of enthusiasm shown by Britain and France for Italy's claim to Dalmatia which would strengthen Italy as a naval power at the expense of their own protégé Yugoslavia.

In Italy itself there were plenty of people, including some nationalists, willing to give up Dalmatia in exchange for Fiume. The army preferred this solution but the navy had developed a doctrine which held that the Dalmatian coast, with its labyrinth of islands and inlets, should not be left in the hands of a potential enemy. They considered the Adriatic an 'Italian Gulf' and this idea was seized by the nationalists to strengthen their sentimental claim to the Dalmatian cities on which Venice had left the mark of her civilization.

In the controversy over Fiume versus Dalmatia the government was divided. Orlando preferred Fiume, but his foreign minister Sonnino was adamant in favour of Dalmatia. At the Peace Conference the Italians asked for both, though Orlando almost certainly intended to give up some of the Dalmatian claims in the course of the negotiations. He reckoned without Wilson and Sonnino. Wilson was determined to make the Adriatic Question the test case for his ideas about open diplomacy. He had waived the nationalities principle in favour of a strategic frontier for Italy on the Brenner (which gave Italy some 250,000 German-speaking subjects) but he made a moral issue of Dalmatia. As for Fiume, he thought the Italians might, on the same ground, claim sovereignty over Brooklyn. Against him stood Sonnino, a cultivated, old-fashioned Tuscan gentleman, as high-principled and unbending in his way as Woodrow Wilson. Sonnino had been foreign minister since 1914 and had himself negotiated the Treaty of London. That treaty was his grand achievement, his one reason for wanting Italy to enter the war. In his view Italy had not been fighting for democracy (as Bissolati and Salvemini believed), still less for imperialistic aggrandisement. She had been fighting simply to complete the work of the Risorgimento.

Sonnino, like many people in Italy, failed to see how the balance of power had altered in Europe, to Italy's disadvantage, through the events of 1917 and 1918. Czarist Russia and Habsburg Austria were gone. The United States, a new power with a different ethos and different ambitions, had entered the scene. In this new context Italy's diplomatic strength was almost nil. She no longer tipped the scales between east and west in Europe for, without Austria, she had no leverage. Sonnino's world was shattered. Wilson overshadowed the Peace Conference and he was determined that the wicked balance-of-power game should never be played again. The Italians scandalized him. He asked them what they meant by 'sacred egoism' and complained that Italy had entered the war 'out of cold-blooded calculation', which was true of the government but certainly not of the nation. The Italian public was bewildered. A few months earlier it had welcomed President Wilson as the Mazzini of the twentieth century.

Lloyd George and Clemenceau were less priggish. Clemenceau pointed out that 'we none of us started this war as liberators', while Lloyd George tried to make Wilson see that, when all was said and done, the Italians had fought with the Allies whereas the Serbs and Croats had fought against them. Since the United States had not signed the Treaty of London Wilson refused to recognize it but Lloyd George and Clemenceau could not repudiate it outright. Small wonder if Sonnino felt that, in a hostile world, his only strength lay in this 'scrap of paper'. With more acumen Orlando realized that the Treaty was now merely a blueprint for maximum concessions, not a guarantee that they would be made. He was just about to climb down when Wilson made the extraordinary move of appealing to the Italian people directly over the heads of their government. He had been acclaimed with enthusiasm in Italy in January 1919 and seems to have imagined that the nation was as angry as he with its 'wicked' representatives in Paris. Orlando and Sonnino left the Peace Conference in a fury and were welcomed in Italy, not surprisingly, as the victims of a plot to humiliate the nation.

Taken in themselves Wilson's proposals were not unreasonable. The so-called Wilson line offered the Italians more than they ultimately received when they signed the Treaty of Rapallo with Yugoslavia in 1920. But even Italian democrats were disconcerted by Wilson's refusal to cede Fiume and by his extraordinary approach. Salvemini thought he had picked on Italy alone as the victim of his moral principles. The misunderstanding was never completely ironed out. It was Italy's first brush with Anglo-Saxon self-righteousness. John Maynard Keynes, who attended the Peace Conference, thought the language barrier prevented understanding between the peacemakers. Orlando spoke no English (but Sonnino's mother was a Scotswoman) and Wilson spoke no French. In fact there was a spiritual incommunicability between the Italians and Wilson which no interpreter could bridge. Lloyd George and Clemenceau did not try. Those two astonishing characters understood the old diplomacy better than the new. They were not out to help Wilson achieve his starry-eyed vision of international justice, while they saw much to be gained for their respective nations from taking advantage of the Italians' ineptitude. Italy had great-power ambitions but her negotiators in Paris did not behave like the representatives of a great power responsible for settling world affairs. Orlando actually boasted that he took no interest in matters which did not concern Italy directly and only intervened when he saw the chance to bring grist to Italy's mill. His behaviour made one English witness, Harold Nicolson, observe that the Italians were 'frankly out for loot'. But in the end it was Britain and France who got most of the booty when they quietly divided Germany's African colonies between them. None the less, in world opinion, the Italians stood branded as greedy and cynical.

Out of the tragicomedy in Paris a new world order was born which contained the seeds of fascism. The Italians suffered further diplomatic humiliations but eventually received a good deal of what they had asked, except Dalmatia and Fiume, which D'Annunzio later seized. It was the atmosphere of the Peace Conference rather than the substance of the treaties that made it possible for Italian nationalists to propagate the doctrine of Italy's 'mutilated victory'. Possibly no treaty would have suited them. Unfortunately the democratic interventionists, whose job it should have been to soothe the nation's ruffled pride, were put out of the running at an early stage of the peace talks. Bissolati resigned from the government when Italy demanded Dalmatia and was howled down at a public meeting in Milan for suggesting that she should give up Fiume and the Alto Adige as well. It was a foolish proposal which only served to discredit the democrats as 'renouncers' and showed that, for all their prophetic vision, these radicals were moralists rather than politicians. The fact was that although Italy's most important newspaper, *Il Corriere della Sera,* championed the cause of friendship with Yugoslavia, there was no real political backing for such a policy. The catholics were indifferent. To be effective it would have required the support of the socialists but that party was not at all impressed by Wilson's appeal for international friendship and co-operation. It was Lenin, not Wilson, who held the socialists' attention immediately after the war.

5   Into fascism

THE BOLSHEVIK REVOLUTION had a hypnotic effect upon Italian socialists. While they totally lacked the strength or the resolution to bring about a similar upheaval in Italy, they persuaded themselves that it was imminent. They saw the revolutionary tide rolling towards Italy from eastern Europe and thought they could see analogies between conditions in Italy and pre-war Russia. Both were peasant nations with a late-starting industry and an organized working-class élite. In Italy, as in Russia, insurrection was endemic among both the workers and the rural proletariat. Antonio Gramsci, who became one of the founders of the Italian Communist Party in 1921, believed that revolution had succeeded in Russia because the leaders had been able to co-ordinate the two movements, getting the peasants to follow when the workers gave the lead. He thought this strategy could be applied to Italy and tried to put it into effect by starting a movement among the engineering workers in Turin to convert the wartime factory councils (set up by management) into revolutionary workers' committees. The movement was only partially successful for it never quite convinced the unions whose influence it tended to supplant. Though it never spread much beyond Turin it gave rise to a brief and impassioned struggle for workers' control of management, culminating in the celebrated clock strike at the Fiat motor works in April 1920. This strike (against the imposition of daylight saving) was the last of a series of truly political strikes on the issue of workers' control. It failed and the agitations which followed were of a more conventional character, sparked off by the economic crisis which struck Italy in the autumn of 1920.

Gramsci was aware of the difficulty of co-ordinating rural and industrial insurrection and always feared that the two might go off separately without provoking revolution. This is substantially what happened in Italy during the 'red years' of 1919 and 1920. Probably the only time when revolution might have succeeded in Italy was in the winter of 1917, when demoralization and war-weariness could perhaps have been turned to account by a resolute group of men; but when the fortunes of war and the temper of the country changed after Caporetto and a patriotic revival set in, the opportunity was gone. Henceforth neither the international context nor the economic reality of Italy (no subcontinent, like Russia, but a vulnerable peninsula dependent on imports) made revolution possible.

Long after external conditions favourable to revolution had vanished, the insurrectional mood survived, and the post-war years were punctuated by bread riots, industrial strikes, rural agitation and peasant squattings on the land that had been promised to the ex-servicemen. Such a period of tumult had not been seen in Italy since 1898. Between April and September 1920 there were 140 clashes with the police. Railwaymen and seamen refused to carry troops against the workers. A special police corps was created to cope with the situation and the socialists reported 320 dead.

Chronic agitation caused the socialist leaders and their Soviet mentors to think that revolution was at hand, and Lenin and Trotsky actually reproached the socialists for 'losing' Mussolini, whom they considered the man best qualified to bring it about. Dissatisfaction with the performance of the Italian socialists caused Lenin to set them hard terms for admission to the Third International in 1919. Among his twenty-one conditions was the injunction to change the party's name from socialist to communist and the order to expel the reformists, including Turati who had been its founding father. Serrati and the maximalist leaders refused these conditions while proclaiming their allegiance to the International. Turati and Treves remained in the party in the name of the quasi-mystical unity of the working classes. It was the communists who broke away at the famous congress in Leghorn in January 1921.[1] Amadeo Bordiga, a Neapolitan mathematician, was the leading personality on the communist side, but the party was born of a fusion between Bordiga's following who centred on his paper *Soviet* published in Naples, and the Turin group of *Ordine Nuovo* which revolved around Gramsci, Togliatti, Tasca and Terracini. These last were brilliant young intellectuals who soon eclipsed the other group. Tasca eventually defected but the others, particularly Gramsci at first and Togliatti later, gave Italian communism the cachet which has made it, circumstances aiding, the most important communist party in the West.

The Leghorn split left a small minority of reformists in uncomfortable association with the maximalists in a much weakened Socialist party which already contained the seeds of a second split. Repudiated by Moscow, it contained to hanker after the Third International and refused to collaborate with any government that represented the despised bourgeoisie. For the people concerned these events were a spiritual drama, for Italian socialism was more akin to a religious movement than anything that had occurred in Italy since the Counter-Reformation. Subtle points of doctrine were argued by the leaders and followed by the rank and file with all the passion of religious controversy. In vain Serrati pleaded with the Russians that Italian reformists were not heretics but observers of the true faith. As Pietro Nenni, later to be the party's leader, observed, the party had become a church and while the wrangling went on the opportunity for action slipped by. This was the more tragic because conditions favourable to the democratic growth and consolidation of socialism existed in Italy at the time.

In 1919 the socialists controlled a third of the provincial councils. Municipal government in important cities such as Milan, Genoa and Bologna was in their hands and the network of their leagues, labour chambers and co-operatives spread over most of north and central Italy. The General Confederation of Labour, which was allied to the Socialist party by a pact, had seen its membership rise from under 300,000 before the war to over two million. Finally at the election of November 1919 the socialists found themselves, with 156 deputies, the biggest organized group in Parliament. Altogether the potential for socialist action was immense.

In most socialist organizations at the provincial level the reformists were predominant but the party's voting and card-holding system

76

were such that this trend was inadequately represented at the centre, where the maximalists prevailed. These doctrinarians were so dazzled by the pattern of events in Russia that they misinterpreted what was going on at home. They saw that the old liberal regime was breaking down under the impact of new forces but they lumped all social classes, other than the industrial and rural proletariat, together under the label 'bourgeois' and thought they were all equally doomed. In reality the Italian middle classes were more resilient and articulated since the war and not all identified themselves with the liberal state. In addition to the old professional élite which had been the dominant class in Italy from 1860 to 1915, there was a new group of financiers and industrialists fully aware of their recently acquired wealth and power; there were also the very numerous ranks of the new poor, fixed-income holders who had been ruined by the inflation. Many of these might have been attracted into the Socialist party had Turati and the reformists been in control.

With incredible ineptitude the socialists kept up the hostility they had kindled during the war years against all but the lowest ranks at the front. Thanks partly to this foolish and cruel attitude the distinction between neutralists (or pacifists) and interventionists was as bitter in 1919 as it had been on the outbreak of war. Officers and even humble soldiers were frequently set upon in the streets by a socialist hue and cry. At the time some two hundred thousand demobilized draft officers were coming home to inflation and a society which offered them neither work nor a pension nor social status comparable to what they had enjoyed under arms. Men from middle-class homes, whose standard of living had deteriorated drastically since the war, were derided in public by the workers whose condition, in northern Italy, had improved. The rancour of this class conflict produced the climate in which fascism was born. Men viewed the humiliations inflicted upon Italy by her allies in the light of their personal frustrations and from the ranks of discontented war veterans and ex-interventionists Mussolini recruited the forces he needed for his grand design.

The fascist movement was founded in Milan on 23 March 1919 when Mussolini invited a few score of sympathizers to a meeting in the premises of the Alliance of Industry and Commerce in Piazza San Sepolcro. The Sansepolcristi included some futurist intellectuals and ex-revolutionary syndicalists but the mass of adherents at this stage came from the associations of Arditi. The Arditi were special commando forces used in the first world war with functions and a status similar to those of the parachutists or the marines in World War II. Their creed was violence, their emblem the skull and cross-bones and their slogan could be politely translated 'Who cares?' They were out for adventure and were as much attracted by D'Annunzio – who made use of them to seize Fiume in September 1919 – as by Mussolini. The Arditi had their own rites and symbols. They wore black shirts and carried hand grenades and indulged in a sort of shouted dialogue between the commander and his troops. This folk-lore and choreography, embellished by D'Annunzio, were taken over by the fascists and helped them to capture the imagination of Italian youth.

At first the movement had neither doctrine nor ideology and its programme was an incredible mixture of revolutionary syndicalism and free-trade liberalism. The fascists declared themselves republican and anticlerical. They wanted to abolish the Senate, confiscate ecclesiastical property and impose a capital levy and a progressive tax on wealth. They demanded an eight-hour day for the workers and compulsory insurance and said they would abolish every form of state control over the economy. Mussolini announced that fascism was to be an anti-party and that men must be freed from the tyranny of the party card. This was a reference to the socialist practice of making party membership a condition for receiving jobs through the socialist leagues; ironically it was socialism that gave Mussolini a model of party tyranny.

The foreign policy he outlined to the Sansepolcristi was nationalist and imperialist though he was talking as yet in terms of economic and 'spiritual' expansion. The League of Nations might be useful if it helped national integration (i.e. allowed Italy to swallow Dalmatia and Fiume) but it was not to be used by the rich nations to cheat the poor. In reality there was only one item of the programme that really mattered to Mussolini. In the name of the interventionists who had led Italy to war and victory he claimed the right for the fascists to take over from the tottering liberal state.

Mussolini's programme was devised to attract both workers and employers, whichever would swallow the bait. The workers looked strong in 1919 and Mussolini perhaps thought he had an off-chance of rising to power as a tribune of the people. At least the card was worth playing. But the workers showed no interest in his social demagogy for they still had faith in their own party and unions. Encouragement was to come from the other side. The war had favoured the structural concentration of heavy industry protected by state contracts and subsidies. Its owners thought they could prolong this happy state of affairs and retard its conversion to the less profitable uses of peace. They were willing to finance a man and a movement who seemed likely to help them as much as, if not more than, the nationalists. Significantly Mussolini's most substantial backing came from the Perrone brothers, owners of the Ansaldo steel works. Other industrialists followed, as can be deduced from the advertisements in his newspaper *Il Popolo d'Italia*, and with this sort of financial backing Mussolini soon dropped the cause of the workers for that of the 'producers' – by which he claimed at first to mean both employers and workers, as distinct from the 'non-productive parasites of Right and Left'.

Mussolini's relations with big industry were to help him into Parliament. They began at the time of the municipal elections in October 1920. By January 1921 he was writing in praise of capitalism, which he called 'an elaboration of irreplaceable historic values'. Six months later he told Parliament in his maiden speech – he was then a simple deputy – that fascism stood for free-trade liberalism of the Manchester School, and later still he spoke of returning the railways and telegraph to private ownership. By that time the Confederation of Industries was beseeching the King to send for him to form a government. But this is anticipating. The question arises, did Mussolini change his tune in 1920 because he had already received financial backing from big industry or because he hoped for it? The first is more probable though it cannot be proved. The alliance was cemented in 1921 when the industrialists were looking for an ally to protect them from Giolitti's tax reforms, particularly the dreaded registration of bearer bonds.

From the outset the fascist movement was founded upon violence and its first exploit was to wreck the offices of *Avanti* in Milan during the political strikes of April 1919. To contemporaries the movement at first looked marginal and freakish. It lacked popular support and took a severe beating in the election of November 1919. This was the first election to be held in Italy since the war. The outgoing Parliament, at the end of its prolonged mandate, introduced proportional representation and voting by lists. The intention was to free deputies from the influence of local pressure groups. Giolitti thought the reform would make Parliament unmanageable but the liberals who voted it failed to see that it would hurt them by favouring the more closely organized parties with a much wider electoral base. In fact it benefited the socialists, who returned 156 deputies, and the catholics of the *Popolari*, the new Popular party, who returned 100.

The Popular party was founded in January 1919 with the cautious consent of the Church. It grouped together catholics of different trends. Its left wing derived from the old Christian Democrat movement (banned by Pius X as too progressive) and was pacifist, tradeunionist and ferociously anticapitalist. This faction distrusted socialist materialism and competed with the socialists in the sphere of the trade unions and labour leagues, but it favoured a political alliance between the two parties. The Popular party also had a right wing composed of clerical moderates who were socially conservative and were willling to collaborate with the liberals if these would moderate their anticlericalism. The moderates wanted equal status for catholic and state schools, the assurance that divorce would never be introduced into Italian legislation, and more consideration for the Pope. This group had a finger in papal finance through the Banco di Roma and was more influential in the Vatican than the catholic party's centre and left.

The bulk of the Popular party stood in the centre with its founder Luigi Sturzo. Don Sturzo was a Sicilian priest and a man of outstanding moral prestige. He had belonged to the Christian Democrat movement but kept aloof from its quarrel with the Church, devoting himself to the sphere of the catholic trade unions and municipal government. His aim was to enable Italian catholics to pull their weight in politics with a party of their own, which should be autonomous and independent of the ecclesiastical hierarchy. The catholics in Italy had always disliked the centralizing trend of the lay state and the *Popolari* now stood for administrative decentralization and a reform of the bureaucracy. Their social creed derived from catholic sociology and was vaguely corporative; unions, industrial or agricultural, were to reconcile and harmonize the interests of management and labour, of landlord and tenant. The party's main support came from the small farmers and sharecroppers of north and central Italy. It had a wider peasant base in Venetia and in the Po Valley, where the white catholic leagues had long rivalled the red leagues of the socialists.

The weakness of the Popular party lay in the contradictions inherent in its central position, part conservative, part progressive. Sturzo himself was nearer to the Left than to the clerical moderates but he was hampered by the ambiguous attitude of the Papacy towards his party and himself. Benedict XV was in some respects an enlightened pontiff and was willing to allow Sturzo's experiment to proceed, but the Papacy was not deeply interested in its success. The Church's main concern at the time was to enhance the prestige of the Papacy, which appeared to have suffered through the war, particularly with the defeat of Austria. Exclusion from the Peace Conference was a sore point in the Vatican. Benedict therefore began to sound the Italian government for a solution of the Roman question which would improve the political standing of the Pope. His successor Pius XI became convinced that the Church could get better terms from an authoritarian government under Mussolini (who openly declared his contempt for liberal 'prejudices') than it was likely to get from a democratic government which might include some catholics but in which the liberal tradition would still prevail. Cardinal Gasparri, the Pope's Secretary of State, sounded Mussolini, who promised to recognize the temporal sovereignty of the Pope in Rome. When the Cardinal objected that he would never get the

Chamber to approve, Mussolini replied, 'We will change the Chamber.' The Cardinal noted in his diary: 'I realized that with that man, should he get into power, we could conclude.' All this explains how the Popular party, for all its numerical strength and organization, suffered from the same sort of divisions and inhibitions as the Socialists. These too were in an uneasy relationship with their spiritual mentors in Moscow.

Not a single fascist was returned to Parliament in November 1919. The movement fared badly even in Milan, its founding city, and Mussolini almost gave up politics in disgust. His enemies thought his career was over and *Avanti* cracked a feeble joke about his putrefied corpse being found in the canal. Had fascism depended for survival on its programme the movement might have petered out. The various factors, social, cultural, psychological, which had brought it into being – the cult of violence, the disgust with Parliament, the disappointment in the fruits of victory – would hardly have carried it forward but for two exceptional circumstances: the economic crisis which engulfed Italy in 1920, and the political deadlock which brought parliamentary government to a standstill between 1921 and 1922. The first created the opportunity for the fascist squads to come into action and the second enabled Mussolini to deploy his extraordinary talent for exploiting the weakness of his opponents.

The economic crisis stemmed from the United States and came to aggravate the ills inherent in the economic policies adopted at Versailles. No one at the Peace Conference except John Maynard Keynes (and least of all the Italian delegation) had realized that Italy stood in as great need of economic and financial help from her allies after the war as she had done during the conflict. Europe and America were to learn the facts about economic collapse the hard way, and thanks to this lesson Italy was to recover quickly from her defeat in 1943 whereas the victory of 1918 left her prostrate. No sooner was the war over than Britain and the United States cut off their credits, which had kept the lira relatively stable since 1915. The currency collapsed and prices rose to six times above their pre-war level. Italy had depended on her allies for raw materials and, in part, for wheat. Now, though the government was running a costly bread subsidy, there were hunger riots which created a climate of social unrest. The socialists themselves did not like this sort of rioting, which smacked of *jacquerie* and escaped their control. Much of it was fomented by the anarchists under their leader Errico Malatesta. The socialists tried to set up food soviets, which did not work, but for a short time shopkeepers and farmers put themselves unwillingly under the protection of the socialist leagues. The situation created an illusion of socialist power.

As the American recession reached Europe the Italian steel and engineering industries and textiles found themselves in trouble. Unemployment reached 600,000 in 1921, a large figure for the labour force of those days, almost entirely concentrated in the north. In the summer of 1920 the crisis in the steel and engineering sectors, where employers were resisting wage increase demands, led to a series of strikes during which, after an attempted lockout by the employers, the workers took over the factories and tried to run them themselves. The episode is a landmark in Italian social history as important as the general strike in Britain of 1926. For a while neither side was quite certain whether this was a traditional labour dispute or the beginning of revolution. The workers were flying red flags over the factories and using revolutionary language but when representatives of the unions and the socialist party got together in September to decide the next step, the trade unionists insisted upon caution. Soon afterwards the labour dispute was settled with some assistance from Giolitti, who had become prime minister, for the last time, in June 1920. Faithful to his pre-war policy he allowed the strikes to run their course and would not use force against the workers. These were beaten by the inflation which made it possible for employers to grant some wage increases while continuing to lay off redundant labour. Agitation, propped by revolutionary talk, was to continue for a year longer but in fact the workers had lost their battle when the great steel strike was called off in September 1920.

This date marks the beginning of a serious breach between the unions and the Socialist party. Gramsci, who was a lucid observer on the socialist side, saw with misgiving that the country was heading either for revolution or, more probably, towards a devastating conservative reaction. Mussolini had been careful to sympathize with the workers at the beginning of the agitation but now saw that they were beaten, and described the later strikes as the St Vitus dance of marxist epilepsy. Throughout the crucial period of the industrial labour disputes the fascists had taken only a very marginal part in the agitation (sometimes even siding with the workers). Organized *squadrismo* appeared for the first time in September 1920, when fascist squads wrecked a Slav newspaper and other Slav headquarters in Trieste. *Squadrismo* then came into action in a big way during the municipal elections of November 1920 but the legend that the fascist squads had saved Italy from a Bolshevik revolution was invented afterwards.

While the agitation was at its height, in March 1920, the employers set up their own organization, the powerful Confederation of Industries (*Confindustria*), which was to be their strength and protection for many decades not only in their struggles with the labour unions but in their relations with government. From the outset the Confederation was conceived as a political instrument. Its function was to put pressure on government on behalf of employers and, should this fail, to bring the government down, if necessary at the expense of the régime.

By the autumn of 1920 the economic crisis was affecting rural Italy, creating a situation that was to favour the birth of agrarian fascism and give rise to a state of civil war. During the wartime expansion of industry unskilled labourers had flocked to the towns. These men were the first to be turned away when recession came and they now trekked back to their homes in the Po Valley only to find that jobs on the land were controlled by the all-powerful socialist leagues. A displaced and desperate proletariat appeared to help the landowners in their struggle against the leagues. At first the land-owners set up their own armed bands, but they soon found it convenient to turn to the fascists, who could provide them with a mercenary army of terrorists recruited both locally and in the towns, and commanded by young adventurers who fancied themselves in the role of condottieri (they were operating in the territory which had seen the exploits of Caesar Borgia and other Renaissance heroes).

84

These men became known as the *ras*, a title borrowed from the Abyssinian chieftains encountered in the colonial wars. Italo Balbo, Dino Grandi, Leandro Arpinati and Roberto Farinacci were the most powerful of the *ras* and over them Mussolini, at this period, had little or no control. Emilia and Tuscany were the main theatres of the private war conducted by the fascists on behalf of the land-owners, for it was there that the socialists were most firmly entrenched in their 'red baronies'. Bologna was the capital of this socialist en-clave and its conquest became the principal strategic objective of the 'war'. But the fascist raids soon spread to other rural areas in Lom-bardy, Venetia and Apulia, wherever there was a large population of *braccianti* (day-labourers) and where the landowning community included a fair number of small freehold and tenant farmers for these were as bitterly opposed to the socialist leagues as the big landowners. Socialist policy for the land, at the time, was completely doctrinaire and took no account of the *de facto* situation. The socialists proposed collective ownership and co-operatives.

The 'civil war' lasted from the autumn of 1920 to the spring of 1922 but by the middle of 1921 the socialists were on their knees. More than seven hundred of their labour chambers, league head-quarters and co-operatives had been destroyed and over sixty municipal councils had been dissolved by violence. The fascist raids were organized by the *ras* and financed by the landowners but the arms and transport employed were often army stock stolen or even borrowed from the army or the carabinieri. Reserve officers not infrequently took part in the expeditions and sometimes actually commanded the squads. Clearly the fascists could never have suc-ceeded so completely had they not enjoyed the sympathy of the army, the prefects, the magistracy and the police. Just how far the central government inspired or endorsed the behaviour of its pro-vincial agents is more difficult to ascertain. In January 1921 the socialist deputy Giacomo Matteotti denounced Giolitti and the ministry of the interior for their complicity with the fascists, and most historians today agree that an explicit understanding between Giolitti and Mussolini was reached in the autumn of 1920 through the good offices of the prefect of Milan, Lusignoli. The agreement was that

Giolitti would allow the fascist squads to act with relative impunity if the fascists would withdraw their support from D'Annunzio in Fiume.

The Fiume affair was an embarrassment to the government from the start. Orlando, who was prime minister at the end of the war, had encouraged the nationalists by occupying Albania, but his successors Nitti and Giolitti had a more realistic grasp of Italy's international position and saw the need to cultivate better relations with her ex-allies. Nitti (who was prime minister from June 1919 to June 1920) was obsessed by Italy's economic plight and believed that without American aid the population would starve. To curb the nationalists he brought in proportional representation, which was to favour the 'neutralist' socialists and catholics, but his policy enraged the ex-interventionists, who began plotting a military pronunciamento. Plans to seize Split in Dalmatia and set up a republic of the Tre Venezie under the Duke of Aosta were on foot in exalted military circles until a press leak caused them to be dropped. At the same time, in the south, the ex-combatants, exasperated by the government's failure to start distributing the land which had been promised to the soldiers, began talking of a march on Rome. Thus the idea of a coup d'état was in the air some time before D'Annunzio tried it out in Fiume or Mussolini brought it off in Rome.

The signature of the Treaty of St Germain with Austria on 10 September 1919 was the signal for the march on Fiume. The initiative did not come from D'Annunzio but from a Major Reina at the head of a group of grenadiers. At Reina's invitation D'Annunzio took command and entered the town without encountering resistance. The government was too weak to stop a sedition which had the good will of so large a part of the army and the fleet. In Fiume D'Annunzio set up his so-called 'Regency of the Carnaro' where he tried out some of the ideas and techniques, including a corporative constitution, that fascism was later to adopt. All sorts of nationalists, syndicalists and futurists flocked to Fiume, which soon outshone Mussolini's headquarters in Milan. Though he felt obliged to uphold the national hero in his paper, Mussolini did not relish a situation which left him in the shadow and escaped his control. He had every reason to welcome the overtures from Giolitti (who succeeded Nitti in June 1920) and when D'Annunzio turned to him for help he answered that the police were at his heels.

Mussolini's quiet betrayal of D'Annunzio enabled Giolitti to sign the Treaty of Rapallo, which gave Dalmatia to Yugoslavia and made Fiume a free state. 'Italians must not be hypnotized by the Adriatic' was Mussolini's comment in the *Popolo d'Italia*. Henceforth the fascist squads were to turn their attention from the Slav provinces to the areas of agrarian dispute. D'Annunzio left Fiume on 28 December with the bitter comment that the Italians were unworthy of their hero. Mussolini was to make a similar reflection twenty-five years later.

Mussolini's services over Fiume seem to have been influential in deciding Giolitti to hold a premature election in May 1921. Parliament was becoming unmanageable with the liberals divided among themselves. Nitti was personally hostile and Salandra was intriguing with the nationalists on the right. The socialists fanatically refused to co-operate and the catholics asked too high a price for their support. Giolitti dissolved the Chambers with the intention of bringing the fascists into Parliament – they had no deputies there as yet – and intimidating the other groups. His apologists claim that he believed he could tame the fascists and use them as pawns in his old parliamentary game; but more up-to-date criticism suggests that the old man had no such illusion. On the contrary, he had lost faith in liberal democracy and was deliberately creating a situation which would enable the monarchy to save itself if necessary by a coup d'état.

Whatever his motives, the 'infernal' elections (as Nenni called them) of 1921 were a turning-point in Mussolini's career. His fortunes at the time were at a relatively low ebb, for the exploits of the *squadristi* were outside his control and enhanced the prestige of the *ras*. It was the foothold in Parliament which enabled him to get into power by constitutional means seventeen months after the election. Mussolini often bragged that he had the choice of the revolutionary or the parliamentary road, but he lacked physical courage and would never have led a fighting revolution himself.

Had fascism come into power by violence alone its story would have been quite different, for Mussolini would have been the prisoner of the military chiefs and of the *ras*, and fascism would probably have developed along the classical lines of a military dictatorship. It was Giolitti's action in April 1921 which allowed Mussolini to regain control of the movement and, with his thirty-five fascist deputies, come at last legally to power.

The rest of the story is soon told. By April 1922 the fascists were completely victorious in the Po Valley, Tuscany and Liguria. By murder and arson, by sacking and beating and dosing with castor oil, they had driven the socialists from municipal power and broken both the socialist and the catholic leagues. The trade unions, disgusted by the ineptitude of socialist politics, deserted the party which asked such heavy sacrifices of the workers while failing to defend their interests or even their lives. In Parliament it became increasingly difficult to form a government since neither the socialists nor the catholics would collaborate with the liberals, still less join forces to form a government between themselves. Giolitti himself withdrew a month after the 'infamous election' (where fascist violence dominated the polling for the first time). By June 1922 the army chiefs and the big men in the Confederation of Industries were urging the King to bring Mussolini into government. Foolish old liberals like Orlando and Salandra tendered the same advice in the illusion that they, and not Mussolini, could still call the tune. By this time not only reactionary nationalists but constitutional liberals like Croce, Einaudi and Albertini were preaching that the fascists must be brought into government in order to 'normalize' the movement. Long after Mussolini became prime minister and startled the deputies by his offensive language towards Parliament, these and other outstanding liberals clung pathetically or obstinately to this view. They were to change their minds later and some redeemed their reputations by submitting to persecution but these conversions came too late to save anything but conscience.

6   The legacy of fascism

IN THE HALF CENTURY since the advent of fascism Italians have
never ceased to ask themselves exactly what happened and why.
Croce tried to brush aside the twenty years' dictatorship as an
interlude, something foreign to the main theme of Italian history.
For him fascism was a disease which Italy had picked up fortuitously
and cast off without suffering permanent harm. This complacent
view served to justify the reappearance of the old liberal notables
(some of whom had supported fascism at first) on the downfall of
the régime. At the other end of the liberal spectrum Giustino
Fortunato, as early as 1924, saw that fascism was 'not a revolution
but a revelation'. It exposed the weak points of Italian society and of
a governing class which Fortunato considered 'selfish, arid and
cynical'. Centuries of poverty, clerical domination and foreign rule,
he thought, had left the Italians 'bigoted, servile and boastful'. On
this count the ultimate responsibility for fascism went back to the
Council of Trent. Salvemini also believed that fascism sprang from
the inherent weakness of a nation which for nearly three centuries
had stood outside the mainstream of European progress. But
Salvemini overestimated the personal responsibility of Giolitti,
whom he blamed for allowing violence and corruption to spread
from the southern constituencies until they affected the whole of
Italy.

These moralistic or masochistic explanations of fascism are not
fully accepted today any more than Croce's disculpatory answer.
On the fascist side an outstanding historian, Gioacchino Volpe,
thought that fascism was the last phase of the great national up-
thrust from the Renaissance to the Risorgimento, with its emphasis
on primacy. Mussolini's forerunners were Pisacane, Garibaldi and

Mazzini, who had wanted Italy to be great as well as united. Volpe saw fascist Italy as a young state trying to keep up with bigger and tougher neighbours in an age of armed imperialism fostered by big industry and the banks. Substantially, though in a different spirit, this is the view of the contemporary British historian Denis Mack Smith.

For the communists, fascism was the permanent reaction of capitalism to the organized proletariat, a phenomenon that can and does appear in different places at different times. In this context Gramsci saw the workers struggling against fascism as the Jacobins of the twentieth century, in the front line of man's perennial battle for freedom. But in those early days Italian communists refused to make any moral distinction between fascism and socialism, no matter whether democratic or maximalist. The fascists were the right flank, the socialists the left flank of the bourgeois front. During the fascist persecutions of 1924–26 this doctrine brought the Italian communists into conflict with the Third International, which wanted them to co-operate with the socialists and social-democrats against fascism. Among the Italian communist leaders Togliatti alone possessed the quality of *souplesse* which Zinoviev so constantly recommended, and his effective leadership of the party began when Gramsci and Terracina were in prison and it was too late to fight fascism in the open. Togliatti saw quite soon that fascism was something different from traditional bourgeois conser-vatism but neither he nor anyone else among the antifascists imagined that Mussolini's regime could last for two decades. For many years the emigrés thought its collapse was imminent.

It took Mussolini two years to consolidate his hold on the country and transform his government, which at first included liberals and catholics as well as nationalists and fascists, into a personal dictator-ship. The first steps were the creation of the Fascist Grand Council and the conversion of the fascist squads into a national militia. The Chamber he so gravely insulted on becoming prime minister responded by voting him full powers for a year – 'It has got the government it deserves' was Giolitti's comment – and Parliament began the slow decline that was to end in 1926 when all political parties except the fascist PNF were outlawed. Parliamentary elections of a sort were held in 1929 and 1934 (voters were merely asked to approve a list prepared by the Grand Council) and in 1939 the Chamber of Deputies was replaced by a so-called Chamber of Fasces and Corporations. Parliament's eclipse allowed the Grand Council to emerge as the chief consultative organ of the state.

In 1923 an electoral law gave a large bonus to the party with most votes. Among the illustrious liberals who supported this 'reform' were Enrico de Nicola, then president of the Chamber, and the former premier Orlando. Both seem to have believed that liberal conservatives would have a leading place in Mussolini's system. Like Croce and Einaudi, they imagined the function of the liberals was to 'normalize' fascism and make it civilized and respectable. Thanks to the election law, and even more to the brutal intimidation practised by the fascists, the election of 1924 gave the fascist-conservative lists a big majority. Giacomo Matteotti, a reformist socialist deputy, bravely stood up in Parliament to denounce the methods employed by the fascists and promised to produce evidence that would invalidate the election. A few days later he was kidnapped and stabbed to death by fascists led by the notorious *squadrista* Dumini. Mussolini, who had encouraged the use of violence during the election campaign, was widely held to be morally, and perhaps personally, responsible for the murder and the outrage caused a scandal which might have unseated him had not the King come to his rescue. Aghast at the turn things were taking, 123 opposition deputies, mostly liberals, socialists and catholics, decided to boycott Parliament until Matteotti's murderers were brought to justice and the freedoms guaranteed by the Statute restored. The leaders of this boycott – the so-called Aventine secession – Amendola and Albertini (both liberals) seriously imagined that their gesture would persuade the King to dismiss Mussolini, but King Victor Emmanuel complained that the Aventine deputies were a mass of republicans and refused to read the evidence they submitted against Mussolini. Instead he advised the Duce to change his minister of the interior and weather the storm. Mussolini probably owed more to the monarch on this occasion than in

October 1922 when the King refused to proclaim a state of siege in order to stop the fascist march on Rome. Divided, and lacking political leadership – Giolitti would not join it – the Aventine secession remained no more than a moral protest. Mussolini recovered from his panic and soon decided he had nothing to fear. On 3 January 1925 he told Parliament that he alone was responsible for everything that had happened and dared the Chamber to impeach him: 'If fascism has been a criminal association, then I am its head'. 'Forty-eight hours from now', he added, 'the situation will be entirely changed'. The dictatorship dates from that day.

The year 1925 saw the death of a free press in Italy. The owners of *Il Corriere della Sera* and *La Stampa*, the two great liberal papers, were forced to dismiss their editors and appoint government designees. Ugo Ojetti and Curzio Malaparte were not ashamed to take over. *Avanti*, the socialist organ, was suppressed and its editor Pietro Nenni arrested. Henceforth only registered fascist journalists could write. The prime minister's press office became the most important department of government after the police and was later transformed into the ministry for popular culture. It supplied the papers with approved comment as well as information. Economically the journalists became a privileged caste but they contracted habits of servility which, with the return of a free press, they have never wholly cast off. For a while a clandestine antifascist press, communist and radical-socialist, survived thanks to the courage and energy of Gramsci and Gobetti and their friends, but these men were hunted down mercilessly – sometimes even the printers were murdered – and their voices were silenced.[1]

The first wave of political persecutions had sent hundreds of working-class leaders into exile. Now it was the turn of the intellectuals. Amendola and Gobetti died in exile of injuries received at the hands of the fascists. Turati was smuggled out of the country and Salvemini escaped abroad. Scores of antifascist expatriates settled in France, and Paris became the chief centre of radical and socialist opposition to the regime; Togliatti and a few other communists leaders migrated to Moscow, while Sturzo, Count Sforza and Salvemini settled in the United States. But hundreds, indeed thousands of antifascists were not fortunate enough or did not wish to escape. In Paris the leaders of the former Aventine opposition set up a shadow organization, the so-called Antifascist Concentration, but the communists alone kept a network inside Italy, based mainly on cells in the factories. Their organization was retarded at first by ideological disputes, which reflected the great controversy between Trotsky and Stalin, but by 1931 Togliatti had the party under his control and aligned with the International.

In 1929 Salvemini's disciple Carlo Rosselli founded a liberal-socialist movement called Justice and Freedom, which operated from Paris and attracted a dedicated elite. The movement took part in the Spanish Civil War and, under the old risorgimental name of Action Party, played an important part in the Resistance. The Socialists and Actionists had contacts in Italy but of all the anti-fascist parties the communists were by far the most exposed. Of the 4,671 antifascists sentenced by the special courts between 1926 and 1943, 4,030 were communists. Scores of communist agents were hunted down and murdered by the fascists, and some ten thousand antifascist suspects of all parties were sent to the *confino*. With a few exceptions the people sentenced were young men under thirty. For many of them the prisons and *confino* of the fascist regime took the place of university. They graduated after seventeen years to take part in the Resistance. The letters and notebooks of a few of them belong to Italian literature.

The political persecutions led to the setting up of special courts and the redrafting of the penal code. This was the work of the jurist Alfredo Rocco, a former nationalist, whose code – still in force – embodies the authoritarian concept of the state. It introduced the death penalty for attempts on the life of the sovereign and the head of the state (Mussolini) and legislation to safeguard the 'purity of the race'. Since Italy became a republic many sentences given under the *Codice Rocco* have been quashed by the Constitutional Court but, except for the abolition of the death penalty, the code itself has not yet been revised.

The chief instrument of Mussolini's personal power was, of course, the police. As minister of the interior he had the state police under his direct control but its organization was the work of a clever and unscrupulous Chief of Police, Arturo Bocchini, who served him faithfully from 1926 until his death in 1940. Bocchini's aim was to protect Mussolini by keeping the police corps free from infiltration and interference by the Fascist Party while using the information services of the militia and other organs of the PNF, as well as those of the carabinieri who, as a military corps, were more loyal to the King than to Mussolini. Bocchini was responsible for the OVRA, a secret police whose job was to protect the Duce and hunt out anti-fascists at home and abroad. Bocchini built it up with secret-service funds and created a vast network of spies. He and Mussolini used the organization to blackmail and frighten the fascist bosses as well as to hunt down the opposition. Compared to the Nazi police the organization was Bourbonic and clumsy but it was efficient enough to make Italy safe for the dictator. Bocchini's successor, Carmine Senise, another intelligent southerner, betrayed his chief and organized the details of the coup d'état that brought Mussolini to grief in July 1943.[2]

With the King on his side Mussolini could count on the loyalty of the army, which, in the last resort, was the only organ that could have brought him down. In fact his regime lasted just so long as the King stood by him. He fell at last not because the Grand Council turned against him but because the King had decided to get rid of him and double-crossed both the Council and the Duce. But in the heyday of his dictatorship, from 1926 to 1939, Mussolini's control of the state machine was so complete that he hardly needed the party to sustain him. In fact the PNF was always as much a liability as an asset. Its main purpose was to keep the young men happy. The Duce's personal government depended on the control of the police and propaganda and the good will of the army, the business world, the universities and the Church.

The Confederation of Industries supported him from the start and was rewarded by the revocation of the registration of bearer bonds and the dismantling of the labour unions. Only the fascist labour confederation was empowered to negotiate for the workers and, since strikes were illegal and the works committees suppressed,

94

the allegedly corporative structure of labour relations operated to the exclusive advantage of employers. The osmosis between the business world and the régime was perfected in July 1925 when the financier Count Giuseppe Volpi became minister of finance.

Among the intellectuals the most outstanding personality after Croce, the philosopher Giovanni Gentile, gave lustre to Mussolini's first government as minister of education. Gentile believed that the moral and political decadence of Italy stemmed from the cult of individualism developed during the Renaissance. The Risorgimento taught Italians to participate in their social and historical environment, and fascism, in Gentile's view, would continue the good work. This was the gist of the intellectuals' manifesto drawn up by Gentile in April 1925. It affirmed the religious character of fascism and its descent from Mazzini. The manifesto stung Croce to a reply, the famous counter-manifesto signed by forty intellectuals, asserting their faith in the values of freedom, truth and justice which, Croce claimed, had been the soul of Italy for two hundred and fifty years. With this counter-manifesto Croce who was personally hostile to Gentile, at last moved over to the antifascist camp, where his position was singular. Among his scholars a fastidious aristocratic opposition to fascism developed, which produced its fruits towards the end of the dictatorship, but Mussolini had little to fear from their murmurings so long as fortune smiled on him.

In 1931 all but eleven university professors took the oath of allegiance to the régime. To appease the intellectuals Mussolini founded the Italian Academy (modelled on the French Académie). Of the many illustrious characters who accepted membership, Gentile alone was grateful to the Duce and paid for it with his life. In 1944 he thought it his duty to stand by Mussolini as minister of education in the fascist republic of Salò, and a year later he was lynched by partisans. His famous reform of education, introduced in 1923, was an attempt to bring science into greater consideration in Italian schools, but it was only partly successful.

Mussolini's handling of relations with the Church is often considered his masterpiece, but in fact he encountered no real difficulties. The Church went towards him and, in the negotiations for the concordat, Mussolini was no match for his ecclesiastical opponents. The Lateran Pacts, signed on 11 February 1929, were the fruit of long and secret negotiation prepared before Mussolini came to power. Once the Vatican had decided that Mussolini was the man 'sent by Providence', it left no stone unturned to smooth his way. Ecclesiastical pressure was used to remove Sturzo from the leadership of the Popular party in 1923 and the party itself was abandoned to its fate when it turned against Mussolini in 1925.

The concordat with Italy was the crowning achievement of Pius XI's policy, which aimed at negotiating concordats with all the catholic powers. The concessions made by Italy were of immense importance for the future. The Italian state became the secular arm of the Church. It was to punish renegade priests with the loss of civil rights. Catholic schools were given state recognition and religious instruction became obligatory in state schools in the higher forms as well as the elementary. For Mussolini the hardest concession was state recognition of religious marriage. To show the fascists that this was necessary he married Donna Rachele – who had already given him several children – in church.[3]

The Treaty recognized the Pope as sovereign of an independent state, the Vatican City, whose neutrality and inviolability were guaranteed. The financial clauses included an indemnity of 750,000,000 lire in cash and another 1,000 million lire in state bonds. There were also important fiscal exemptions and other privileges, which enabled the Vatican to build up a huge financial empire as a substitute for its lost temporal power. The terms of the concordat implied that the Italian state recognized, instead of merely tolerating, the Church's claim to share in the duties of education and welfare which were to become the formal justification of its financial power. At the same time certain zones of influence, such as Catholic Action and the catholic university, were fenced off from interference by the fascist régime and behind this protective barrier the catholic world concentrated on preparing its lay cadres. Mussolini himself, like most of the fascist leaders, remained fundamentally anticlerical and it was only after the régime collapsed that Italians were able to see how much the Church had had the better part of the bargain.

But in 1929 the 'reconciliation' was of immense value to the dictator and quite restored his international prestige, which had been smirched by the Matteotti affair.

From the beginning Mussolini enjoyed the good will of the Anglo-Saxon powers. In Britain Austen Chamberlain and even Winston Churchill sincerely admired him and Lady Chamberlain was honoured to wear the fascist badge. The friendship of Britain and America was invaluable to Mussolini in consolidating his regime, as Salvemini never tired of pointing out. The status of Italian immigrants in the United States improved radically as a consequence of the esteem shown for the dictator by American politicians and the press. The anti-French bias of his foreign policy was a factor in securing the sympathy of British politicians but the relationship with Britain was based on false premises and mutual ignorance. It developed into a love-hate relationship, and an anti-British polemic became the *leit-motif* of Mussolini's regime.

When Britain turned against him over the Abyssinian war the Duce was sincerely surprised. Until then his foreign policy had been conditioned by traditional balance-of-power concepts; these led him to distrust the new Germany, which appeared to threaten Italy from the East. Hitler's early admiration for the Duce was not returned. Mussolini considered the Führer a 'sexual degenerate' and thought his anti-Jewish persecutions were mad. When Hitler seemed on the point of invading Austria after the murder of Dollfuss in July 1934 Mussolini mobilized his divisions on the Brenner. The decision to invade Abyssinia was taken in 1935 because he believed he would have to fight Germany in two or three years' time.

The Abyssinian war evoked the same kind of patriotic and popular enthusiasm that had sustained the Libyan war of 1911–12. Pius XI approved the adventure, which seemed an opportunity to implement his policy of missionary expansion. In Milan cathedral Cardinal Schuster blessed the standards that were 'to carry the cross of Christ to Ethiopia'. The monarchy and the generals were agog. For the workers the war was a chance to escape from unemployment – there was a recession in Italy at the time – and even the peasants went willingly on the assumption they were to receive farms. Not a few antifascist exiles, including the socialist Arturo Labriola, wrote to Mussolini to offer their support.

Mussolini thought he could count on the friendly neutrality of Britain and France. The three powers had signed an agreement at Stresa in April 1935 to keep watch on German and Soviet expansion in eastern Europe. But the Duce failed to anticipate the complex reaction his invasion of Abyssinia evoked in Britain. His flouting of the League of Nations was a challenge to British interests. Some British historians believe he could have had Ethiopia without fighting for it had he been a better diplomatist, but the fact is he did not want it that way. What he needed was the glory, not the fruits, of victory. His régime, founded on rodomontade, could only survive through war even though war, in the end, was fatal to it. His popularity reached its apex as the nation lashed itself into a fury over the sanctions voted by the League of Nations in October 1935.

The western powers had supposed that this war, like Italy's earlier colonial adventures, would be difficult and long, but Italy sent an army of 400,000 men to East Africa the biggest colonial expedition in history, and the war was brilliantly and cruelly conducted by Badoglio and Graziani, who completed the conquest in seven months. German theoreticians studied their strategy as a model for the future blitzkrieg. Addis Ababa fell on 6 May 1936 and King Victor Emmanuel was proclaimed Emperor of Ethiopia on 9 May. The war is thought to have cost the Abyssinians nearly 800,000 dead. Italian losses have been reckoned at 120,000.

Mussolini's decline starts with the outbreak of the Spanish Civil War. Until 1935 his foreign policy sought to prevent the union of Germany and Austria and to parry German penetration in the Balkans, which threatened Italian interests there and menaced her position in the Adriatic, where Mussolini had secured the annexation of Fiume and a protectorate over Albania. After the conquest of Abyssinia ideological motives got the better of *realpolitik*. A Popular Front reaction to the dictatorships was developing in Europe, and in France Léon Blum became prime minister in place of the pro-fascist Laval – a fact of some importance to the Italian emigrés. Britain and France refused to recognize Italy's

Ethiopian empire and Mussolini found himself drawn into the fatal embrace of his ever admiring friend Hitler. Henceforth his foreign policy became a desperate race to keep up with a much too powerful ally. Under the stress Mussolini began to lose contact with reality, and signs of instability appear in his conduct.

The Spanish war acted as a catalyst to fascist and antifascist discontent. It brought new hope and courage to the exiles in Paris, among whom it strengthened the influence of the communists. In 1934 the communist and socialist parties in exile had made a pact which reflected the Popular Front orientation of the International. The war meant that the Italians were no longer isolated in their struggle against fascism. Their contribution to the International Brigades in Spain was outstanding. Communists, socialists, anarchists, republicans and followers of Rosselli's movement Justice and Freedom flocked to Spain. At Guadalajara they sustained the brunt of the battle against a 'volunteer' corps from Italy commanded by General Roatta. It was a rehearsal for the civil war between fascism and the Resistance at home. 'Today in Spain, tomorrow in Italy' became Rosselli's slogan. It infuriated Mussolini, who arranged to have the Rosselli brothers murdered in France.

Fascist Italy sent 50,000 'volunteers' to fight in Spain but the enthusiasm that had sustained the Abyssinian war could not be revived. What did revive was the fighting spirit of the industrial workers in the north. After ten years of apathy they turned the factories once more into centres of opposition to the régime. The great ideological showdown in Spain and the new vigour displayed by communist and socialist activists were responsible for the change.

On the fascist front itself many young idealists – as well as older romantics – were disconcerted to see the régime fighting on the side of reaction and clerical obscurantism in Spain and against the principles of social progress for which they naïvely believed the fascist revolution stood. Many a young man and woman started on the 'long march' that was to lead them from fascism to communism.[4] Catholic intellectuals also began to criticize the Church's attitude to the war, which seemed to herald the advent of a Spanish type of clerical fascism in Italy. Even the antifascist intellectuals of Croce's school were roused by the general ferment. In short, all the forces that were to take part in the Resistance were awakened by the Spanish Civil War.

Italy's participation in it was costly and unproductive yet as soon as the war was over Mussolini told his generals he must 'look for something else'. The propaganda machine was ordered to stage a campaign for the 'restitution' of Nice, Corsica and Tunisia, and the Duce himself climbed onto a gun to tell the world he was ready to mobilize eight million bayonets. In reality, as the army chiefs knew and tried to tell him, Italy was quite unprepared for war at a European level and Italian industry was not geared to produce a war potential on the scale of the big industrial powers. In a rare moment of lucidity Mussolini told Hitler in 1939 that Italy would not be ready for war for at least three years, but Hitler was not interested in Mussolini's calculations. Although the two had signed an offensive-defensive alliance (the so-called 'Pact of Steel'), Hitler invaded Poland in September 1939 without advising his friend.

When World War II broke out, the King, the army chiefs and the old fascist *ras* were in favour of neutrality. Italy appeared to be almost in the same bargaining position she had enjoyed in 1914–15. She had taken the precaution of annexing Albania when Hitler invaded Czechoslovakia in 1938. There was no advantage to be had by plunging into the mêlée. But Mussolini was determined that Italy should keep faith with Germany although Hitler assured the Italians their help was not required. He seems to have been genuinely obsessed by the idea that the Italians must show themselves capable of 'nordic' loyalty and he was afraid that the war might end before Italy had joined. To miss the spoils and the fighting, he believed, would be fatal to his régime. Thus, when the French army collapsed, he declared war on France and Britain on 10 June 1940 without consulting the army chiefs. 'I need two thousand dead to sit at the peace table' was his cynical explanation. It seems to have satisfied the King and the generals, for no one made a move to stop him.

Mussolini's declaration of war sent a cold chill through the nation, but it aroused no protest. Like almost everyone else on the Continent in June 1940, the Italians supposed the war was virtually over. The German alliance was not at all popular, particularly since Mussolini had felt obliged to imitate Hitler's anti-Jewish measures. His persecution of the Jews aroused genuine disgust and dismay and finally alienated the good will of the Church. Most people, including perhaps the Duce himself, were afraid of a German victory and many began to realize that they were in the hands of a paranoiac. As the military disasters piled up over the next two years and the German alliance became more oppressive, the population woke up to the fact that fascism had been a gigantic bluff. The only thing that had worked efficiently under the régime was the Duce's propaganda machine, which had concealed the truth from everyone – the Duce himself came to believe his own falsehoods – until it was too late.

Instead of a brief skirmish across the border, Mussolini found himself drawn into an adventure of incredible proportions. From East Africa to Tunisia, from the Balkans to the Don, the Italians were fighting on five different fronts in the worst possible conditions of equipment, training and leadership, and this colossal war effort was sustained by a population already suffering privations as a result of the Duce's policy of economic self-sufficiency, which deprived the country of vital imports. A nation short of calories, a navy without fuel and a war industry lacking raw materials were the sinews of Mussolini's war. It is a tribute to the toughness of the Italians that it took three years for the system to break down. In October 1940 Mussolini invaded Greece, gratuitously, to parry the German penetration of Rumania. This was to have been his 'parallel war' but it ended in the humiliation of having to ask for German help. The Axis partners carved up Yugoslavia but could not hold it against Tito's partisans, and King Victor Emmanuel's cousin, the Duke of Spoleto, never dared to claim his ephemeral kingdom of Croatia. Even more gratuitously, Mussolini sent an army to Russia in November 1942 though Hitler only asked for three Alpine divisions. This was the most tragic and criminal of the Duce's military follies. Only a fraction of this army came home – some to join the Resistance – and ten years later Italians were still asking for news of the 60,000 lost men whose fate has never been ascertained. By May 1943 all Italy's African possessions were lost. The army in East Africa, cut off from the home country and poorly armed, capitulated in November 1942 leaving 300,000 prisoners in British hands. The army in North Africa, routed at El Alamein, was lost with the fall of Tunis and Bizerte.

The first signs of collapse on the home front were the strikes which broke out in northern Italy in March 1943. They began in Turin, the city which had rebelled against World War I in 1917. The strikes were both social and political. Food was short, prices were rising and workers were on a twelve-hour day. The movement was organized by the communists who had formed a committee with the other parties of the Left. The first strike 'for bread, for peace and for freedom' began at the Fiat works on 5 March; immediately the movement spread to Milan and the smaller industrial centres of Lombardy and Piedmont and thence to Emilia and Romagna. Farmers in the Po Valley and students in Rome joined the agitation. Reports reached the King that Mussolini failed to appreciate the anti-war character of the strikes.

Mussolini's prestige could not survive shattering military defeat. By the spring of 1943 it was clear to everyone, including the fascist leaders, that the Duce's conduct of the war was disastrous, and complicated intrigues were on foot at various levels to relieve him of the supreme command. The King and General Ambrosio, the Chief of Staff, were deterred only by the hope that Mussolini might still use his influence with Hitler to get permission for Italy to negotiate a separate peace. This hope faded after the meeting with the Führer on 17 July 1943 (shortly after the Allied landings in Sicily) when Mussolini was cowed and failed to speak. The unhappy meeting of Feltre signed the Duce's fate, but the King still thought he required a constitutional pretext to get rid of his prime minister, for he always clung to the fiction that the Statute of 1848 was still in force.

Dino Grandi, president of the Chamber of Fasces and leader of a moderate *Fronde* against Mussolini in the PNF, supplied the King with a pretext. He persuaded Mussolini to call the Grand Council (which had not met since 1939) and presented an ambiguously worded motion inviting the King to take back the supreme command. Nineteen of the twenty-nine people present at that dramatic meeting voted for this motion without realizing that they were voting their own doom. Everyone concerned in this drama, the King, the generals, Mussolini and the leaders of the fascist *Fronde*, were the victims of self-deception. The basic, fundamental illusion which inspired the King, the generals and Grandi was the belief that Britain and America were planning an offensive in the Balkans with a view to preventing the Russians from establishing their influence there, and that the Western Allies would welcome an understanding with Italy (and eventually with Hungary and Rumania) to keep the Russians away from the Mediterranean. Behind this illusion was the utter failure to understand the ideological passion which had enabled Britain to sustain her incredible war effort and which inspired the United States.

Mussolini's illusion was the belief that he could some day persuade Hitler to make terms with Russia and concentrate his war effort on the Mediterranean sector. In spite of the warnings of his entourage, Mussolini never expected to be dismissed and arrested by the King. With more perspicacity than the fascist *ras* he told the Grand Council that it was not his own head that Churchill and Roosevelt wanted but to degrade Italy from the condition of a Mediterranean power. 'Any peace without me' he told them, 'will be a diktat.' Mussolini did not take the Grand Council meeting too seriously. Under the fascist constitution it had no deliberative powers and Mussolini rightly believed that, without him, the Fascist party would crumble away. His real mistake was to trust the King.

On the afternoon of 25 July 1943, the Duce was arrested on the doorstep of the King's villa and whisked away in an ambulance. A few minutes later the Italians were told that Marshal Badoglio had become prime minister of a military and technical government. Badoglio's message to the nation, written by the old liberal premier Orlando, said: 'The war goes on'.

18 The pre-eminence of Italian films has been a post-war phenomenon. Visconti directed *The Leopard*, from Lampedusa's famous novel; the scene above shows Fabrizio, Prince of Salina, dancing with Don Calogero's daughter (Claudia Cardinale).

19 The *Giostra del Saracino*, or 'Joust of the Saracen', at Arezzo – a popular festival of dance and mime, with its roots in the Middle Ages.

20, 21 *Above, left*: Detail from the bronze doors of St Peter's, by Manzù, showing Pope John XXIII greeting Cardinal Rugambwa of Tanzania at the IInd Vatican Council. *Above, right*: Horse and rider, a favourite theme of Marino Marini.

22 *Below, left*: The Palazzo dello
Sport, Rome, is one of this sport-
obsessed nation's more notable
new buildings. Designed by
Marcello Piacentini and Pier Luigi
Nervi, it seats 15,000 spectators.

23 In building and civil
engineering, modern Italian
achievement ranks very high.
Italian-built factories, dams,
aqueducts and roads can be found
all over the world. *Above, right*:
The Pirelli building in Milan is a
striking example; 127 metres in
height, it was designed in 1956 by
Gio Ponti.

24 Real symbol of contemporary
Italy are the motorways. Costly,
something of a status symbol, they
may nevertheless perform a
valuable function in linking the
north and the south. *Right*:
A section of the Autostrada del
Sole in the Appenines, between
Florence and Bologna.

25 Even such an old-established industry as vine-growing is now adopting modern methods. *Left*: Spraying vines with pesticide by a motor-driven pump.

26 *Below*: Agricultural chemical factory in Sicily, one member of the great Montecatini–Edison chemical combine.

27 Part of the Fiat assembly line in Turin. Here some $1\frac{1}{2}$ million cars and trucks are produced per year by 160,000 workers, and the city, with its population of one million, is in effect the feudal domain of the Fiat company.

28 Uranium-fuelled reactor of the 'swimming pool' type at Saluggia, Piedmont. This is a centre for research into the peaceful uses of nuclear energy.

29–32 Unskilled labourers migrating to the north from the south often find neither job nor housing. The 'shanty town' shown opposite is in Turin, and contrasts strikingly with the new and well-planned, private-enterprise housing development at Potenza (*opposite, below*). *Above*: Nursery school at Ivrea for children of Olivetti's employees – one example of the industrial paternalism that is the modern equivalent of the old *signorie*. *Below*: In spite of clenched fists and 'Viva Mao', student revolt is not exclusively marxist – rather a protest, anarchic, uncontrolled but genuine, against the authoritarianism of Italian society and Italian universities.

33, 34 'Domestic fury and fierce civil strife shall cumber all the parts of Italy.' Mark Antony's prophecy was recalled by the riots and strikes of 1969. Riot police with plastic shields (and where but in Italy could such things be so decorative?) are a commonplace today; less common is the deliberate burning, by their inhabitants, of the wretched shacks that some of Rome's slum-dwellers live in. 'We don't want the moon,' their poster reads, 'just decent housing at a fair price.' And this, one of the basic rights of a citizen, no government has yet been able to provide them.

7   Birth of the republic

THE PERIOD THAT FOLLOWED the collapse of Mussolini's dictatorship was to be as decisive for Italy and as dramatic as the crucial
years 1919 to 1922. Fascism went out, as it had come in, by violence;
but this time the civil war was fought in the context of a general
conflagration. Once again social revolution, or at least the hope of a
new social era, came within sight of the workers, but again the
mirage faded. The régime that was installed with the republic had
little in common with fascism – its style in particular was totally
different – but it was none the less a bourgeois restoration.

At the news of Mussolini's downfall, in July 1943, there was
rejoicing all over Italy and everywhere the emblems of fascism were
torn down, but among the governing class few people, except
perhaps the Duce himself, had realized how completely the régime
was embodied in his person. The disintegration overnight of the
entire fascist apparatus took the King by surprise, as it astonished
the Germans and the Allies. Mussolini, confined on the island of
Ponza, where so many of his victims had languished, reflected that
his system had collapsed and that his fall was irrevocable. Like
everyone else in Italy he thought that fascism had died painlessly.
Certainly he did not expect, still less did he desire, to be rescued and
re-installed by the Germans.

For the King and the generals the next move was more tricky.
Their aim was to make peace with the Allies without bringing
retribution from the Germans. Speed was essential to the success of
this operation but their own fears and the diffidence of the Allies
made speed impossible. Churchill had told the Italians through the
BBC that 'one man and one man alone' was held responsible for

Italy's participation in the war. Now that that man was removed, Badoglio and the King supposed that the verdict of unconditional surrender, decreed by Churchill and Roosevelt, no longer applied to Italy. They seriously hoped to be granted the status of neutrality for they still firmly believed that the Allies' next move would be in the Balkans (to forestall the Russians) and they expected to negotiate a proper treaty, territorial clauses and all.

The Allies had no such intention. They required the use of the Italian airfields and wanted Italian help against the Germans. This, in Churchill's view, was to be the price of Italy's 'passage back'. Undoubtedly the Italian view was naïve and reflected the same sort of moral irresponsibility that had characterized the conduct of Italy's rulers in World War I. But the Allies were also reticent, for their plans concerning the development of the war in Italy were too appalling (from an Italian viewpoint) to be revealed, quite apart from the question of military secrecy. The negotiations dragged on unhappily for three weeks in an atmosphere of deep suspicion on the side of the Allies and increasing fear of the German reaction among the Italians. When the armistice was signed on 3 September the Germans had had time to bring up their strength in Italy from seven divisions to seventeen, and these were disposed to encapsulate the Italian forces in the country. The plan to land an Allied airborne division in Rome could not be executed and the landing 'south of Rome' – the Italians had pleaded in vain for a landing in central Italy – took place at Salerno, seventy miles south of Naples, on 9 September. For this reason General Eisenhower insisted on the armistice being announced on 8 September although the Italian generals, in a panic, were pleading for time.

On the night of 8–9 September the King and his family, the government and the military authorities, including Generals Badoglio and Ambrosio (respectively prime minister and Chief of Staff) left Rome secretly for Pescara, where they embarked for Brindisi leaving the capital undefended and the army in Italy without leadership or intelligible orders. A vague message from Badoglio ordering the troops to cease hostilities against the Allies and 'resist attack from any other source' was given in such a way that it never reached many of the Italian commands. It has been suggested that Badoglio deliberately created this confusion, which left the Italian army in Italy at the mercy of the Germans, in exchange for a safe conduct for the royal party along the two-hundred-mile road to Pescara. No documentary evidence of such an agreement has appeared but the case in its favour is argued persuasively by Ruggero Zangrandi.[1] But even without the added felony of an agreement with the Germans, the King's flight and Badoglio's equivocal orders were a crime against the nation and exposed Italy to the legitimate wrath – and far from legitimate cruelty – of the Germans. More than all King Victor Emmanuel's other errors the flight to Pescara weighed against the monarchy at the referendum of 1946 and cost the Savoy dynasty its throne.

The one thing the Italians had hoped to avoid was a landing in southern Italy, which would turn their country into a battlefield as the Allies fought their way up the peninsula inch by inch. For a poor country densely inhabited this was a terrible punishment. For twenty months Italy was divided into two. North of the battle front the Germans – in no tender mood towards the Italians – were in military occupation. Mussolini, rescued by the German pilot Skorzeny, was made to set up a puppet, or rather a phantom, government in the north of Italy, the ill-famed Fascist Republic of Salò. Southern Italy was under British and American allied military government with priority for political decisions vested in the British. A tiny enclave around Brindisi was left to the King and Badoglio as a pledge of future recognition. It was important to the Allies to maintain the fiction that the authorities who had signed the armistice were the legitimate government of Italy backed by national consensus. But the real Italy, the vital part of the nation, was neither with the King in Brindisi nor with Mussolini in Salò. It was with the Resistance movement, among the partisans in the mountains and the liberation committees in the towns.

Organized military resistance began in the autumn of 1943 in response to the situation created by the armistice. It was backed by a political revival dating from the previous winter which helped to sustain the partisans and gave ideological coherence to the brigades.

By December 1942 all the antifascist parties were operating inside Italy and had formed the alliance that was to give birth to the future liberation committees. The communists were politically and militarily the strongest and best organized, and their Garibaldi brigades comprised more than half the entire partisan force. They were commanded by Luigi Longo, who had experience of guerrilla warfare in Spain. The second largest formation, Justice and Freedom, was affiliated to the Action Party and commanded by Ferruccio Parri. The Catholic brigades were led by Enrico Mattei. The Resistance, however, was something more than a political and military organization. It was also a spontaneous popular movement testifying a deep spiritual and moral revolt. One of its finest episodes was the rising in Naples, when the population drove the German occupants out of the city during five days of heroic street fighting before the Allies entered the town.

But the south had few opportunities to show its spirit, and the Resistance, in the sense of sustained organized action in conditions of special hardship and danger, was characteristic of the north. This does not mean that its members were all northerners. They were recruited partly from the officers and soldiers of the disbanded Italian army and reinforced by fugitives from the draft for the German labour camps and for the army and militia of Salò. By the summer of 1944 there were 100,000 armed partisans operating in north and central Italy. Fighting side by side with the Allies, they helped to clear Florence and the other Tuscan towns. By the end of the war (April 1945) they numbered nearly 250,000. The death roll of the Resistance is impressive. Seventy thousand people connected with it were killed, many after being tortured. These men and women were fighting not only for Italy's moral rehabilitation but for a new social order. For this reason they were distrusted by the conservatives in the Allied Military Government, who had no wish to see a partisan army like Tito's in Italy. It was only after the opening of a second front in Normandy, when the Allies had to remove divisions from Italy, that Churchill decided to give the Italian partisans substantial help. This was conditioned by their reorganization under General Cadorna (son of the commander at

Caporetto) and the undertaking to return their arms to the Allies after the liberation of the north.

The Resistance was a vivifying experience for northern Italy, but Allied Military Government demoralized the south. Italy was granted the status of a co-belligerent nation on the day (13 October 1943) that the King declared war on Germany, but although Churchill was anxious to preserve the monarchy at all costs, he insisted that Italy should be considered technically an enemy country until the final peace was signed. His purpose was to exclude her from the negotiations. The Americans were more generous and would almost certainly have allowed Italy allied status but for British intransigence.

Italy had not much to offer the Allies except her fleet and her air force, both of which passed over to them willingly at the armistice; but the army was in disarray and nothing had been done to get the troops back from Greece, the Balkans and the south of France. Some of these forces tried to resist the Germans after 8 September and the Italian garrison on Cephalonia was massacred. Two Italian divisions in Yugoslavia joined Tito's partisans, but the bulk of the army was captured and 600,000 Italian soldiers were interned in Germany. What remained of the army in southern Italy joined the Allies, who trained and re-equipped a force of 50,000 men. These fought on the eastern sector of the Italian front and in France. Gradually, after months of fighting in Italy, the Allies realized that the Italians were 'paying their way back' not only though the contribution of their armed forces, whether in the regular army or the Resistance, but through the aid and sympathy shown to the Allies by the population. The human qualities of Italian civilization, its grace and kindness and warmth, were a revelation for scores of Britons and Americans who had occasion to turn to the Italians for succour. The prostitution and the black-marketing that followed the Allied armies on their way up from the south could not efface the freshness and humanity of this *rapport*.

In 1943–45 the British still hoped to maintain their dominant role in the Mediterranean and Churchill was reluctant to see Italy rehabilitated. The Americans took a broader view of world strategy and saw Italy as a potential ally, almost a satellite, in the Mediterranean. A compromise between the Allies and the antifascist parties was reached in April 1944. The King was to hand over his powers to his son as Lieutenant-General when the Allies freed Rome. The antifascists were to join the government on their promise not to overthrow the monarchy or introduce social reforms until the war was over. Then the country would be free to choose its form of government.

This agreement, imposed by the Allies, prevented the governments headed by Bonomi and Parri in 1944–45 from getting rid of ex-fascists in industry and the higher ranks of the administration. Only in the north of Italy, where the influence of the CLNAI prevailed for a time, there was a purge of fascist industrialists, and factory councils were set up in some of the big industries. But this 'wind from the north', which alarmed and irritated the Allies, subsided when the Parri ministry fell in December 1945.

Parri had tried not only to purge the Establishment, but to introduce progressive taxes and a capital levy on industry and to allocate raw materials in favour of the small producer. His measures brought down the wrath of the Italian business world and the hostility of the American administrators of aid. Leader of the Action Party, a small group of radical intellectuals, Parri lacked mass support for his Fabian-inspired reforms. He failed to convince the communists and socialists that it was in their interest and that of the workers to keep his government afloat. They let him fall, when the liberals deserted him, without realizing that they were ushering in a long era of undisputed Christian Democrat rule.

Parri had sought to change the moral climate of Italy by removing the corruptors and introducing sweeping reforms, but he greatly under-rated the difficulties. The country was in chaos, its communications shattered, its roads unsafe. A million prisoners of war were coming home to desperate unemployment. Food was in short supply; inflation rampant. Banditry and black-marketeering flourished. At Tombolo deserters from the US army had set up a robbers' republic. Panic seized the middle classes, and class hatred or class fear begat hostility to the Resistance. A movement called l'Uomo Qualunque (the common man) sprang up which derided the new democracy and claimed that Italy had been better off under the old stinker, Mussolini. Unlike Togliatti, Parri failed to see what the Yalta agreements implied for Italy, namely that the country had fallen into the American sphere of influence and therefore the Soviet Union would not come to the aid of a communist revolution there, while, equally, the United States would never let Italy escape from the military and economic system they were building up in Western Europe and the Mediterranean. In these conditions Parri had set himself a hopeless task.

It fell to De Gasperi's first government to hold the referendum that was to choose between the monarchy and a republic. This was the last coalition government to be formed with the six parties of the CLN. The minister of the Interior, Romita, was a socialist. More than any of the antifascist parties the socialists had come to pin their hopes upon the advent of the republic. For the antifascists liberation had been followed by disappointment and humiliation, not least the peace talks which were going badly for Italy. But in June 1946 the Republic appeared as the panacea that was to cure Italy of all her ills. The messianic hope of a new social order which had inspired the Resistance was transferred to the referendum.

With a less brilliant and dedicated minister of the Interior the outcome might possibly have been different, for De Gasperi was careful to keep his own party uncommitted. The results were very close: 12,717,923 votes (54%) for the republic; 10,719,284 against. In the north and centre the republican vote was overwhelming. The monarchists had a clear majority in the south. For a few days Umberto, who had become King on his father's abdication three weeks earlier, tried to contest the results. He received no encouragement from the Allied Commission and at last De Gasperi ordered him to go.

8   Christian Democracy

THE CHRISTIAN DEMOCRACY that came to life in 1943 was more complex than the Popular Party of 1919-26. By and large the old *Popolari* were liberals who had emphasized the separate sovereignty of Church and State, but a common feature of the Catholic trends that developed during the dictatorship was their relative indifference to the political freedoms and their much greater concern with catholic social doctrine. In various degrees these people were 'integrationalists' who believed that politics were the proper business of the Church. Some even held that in the good society political power should stem from her. This was not the view of the party's first great leader, Alcide de Gasperi, who had worked with Sturzo in the Popular Party and, like his old chief, held free political institutions dear. De Gasperi sought to keep the Christian Democrat party as independent as possible of the hierarchy. His ideal, like Sturzo's, was complete autonomy for the Christian Democrats *vis-à-vis* the Church. Some of his collaborators were ex-*Popolari* like himself but the younger men came from Catholic Action and had either belonged to the Catholic Students' Federation (FUCI) or were graduates of the Catholic University in Milan, which had acted as a link between the catholic world and the fascist régime. Its teaching tended to stress the common aim of catholics and fascists and claimed to see their common enemies in the protestants (i.e. the Anglo-Saxon powers) and the Jews. As late as 1939 Amintore Fanfani, a future Christian Democrat leader, was writing in defence of these ideas.[1]

Regional differences, always strong in Italy, affected the Christian Democrats no less than the other mass parties and were as much responsible for ideological trends as the personal bias of individual catholic leaders. Venetia and east Lombardy were always a catholic stronghold and gave the party, as well as the Church, its most reliable cadres. This region, with its farming and mercantile traditions, lacked the dramatic contrasts of Italian society elsewhere. There were no vast estates and the basic industries were on a family scale so that, by and large, the region corresponded to the catholic ideal of a society based on small property and small business, in which the poor were pious and the rich charitable, and both accepted the directives of Catholic Action. In central Italy, on the other hand, the catholics had to compete with a strong socialist and communist tradition harking back to the republicans and the anarchists of the previous century, and further still, perhaps, to the turbulent factions of the medieval communes. Catholicism here tended to be more mystical and more intense. Saint Francis of Assisi and Savonarola both hailed from these parts.

In Florence, after the war, Giorgio La Pira, a Sicilian law professor turned Tuscan mystic, found a terrain on which to build his own municipal brand of catholic integrationalism. As mayor of Florence he ran the city's affairs on the principle that Christian charity begins in the town hall, and when this caused municipal finances to get entangled he left it to the Virgin to straighten them out, which she sometimes did. La Pira and his disciples never quite persuaded the workers of Italy's 'red belt' to give up Marx for the Bible but they did help to build up a special relationship between catholics and communists in a region where local patriotism and a high degree of political awareness go hand in hand.

In the south of Italy catholicism was on a more primitive level with superstition playing a paramount role. The trend had been accentuated by the hardships suffered during the war, and huge sanctuaries sprang up wherever the Madonna was thought to have been specially active in protecting the population. Pompeii and Syracuse became important centres of the pilgrim industry while the reputation of Padre Pio drew tens of thousands to his monastery in the Gargano. This type of society does not favour the growth of a sophisticated political movement, and Christian Democracy in the south tended to rest upon the influence of local notables with their patronage and their clienteles. Immediately after the war the catholic party was less attractive to southerners than the monarch-ists, who bought votes in the open market, or the liberals, who represented the gentry, and, in Sicily, enjoyed the support of the Mafia. In southern Italy, unlike the rest of the country, the bishops were not always on the side of the Christian Democrats and recent research suggests that the catholic party itself encouraged the monarchists to consolidate their influence in Naples and elsewhere with a view to using them as allies.[2]

One movement on the catholic Left stood outside the Christian Democrat fold. The catholic communists saw no inherent contra-diction between catholic doctrine and dialectical or historical materialism, but they felt that the Church's social theory, with its emphasis on small enterprise and class collaboration, was irrelevant to modern industrial society. The movement was short-lived and made little progress towards its aim of representing a revolutionary catholic peasantry in a great federated party of all the workers, but there were some outstanding personalities among its leaders and although most of these drifted into the communist camp, the movement's ideals remained as the latent aspiration of a section of the catholic world. The communists have since made it their business to woo this greater catholic Left.

So varied and heterogeneous were the forces that went to make up Christian Democracy that the movement was more like a coalition or a federation of parties than a political party in the strict sense of the word. The cement which kept the factions together was their common allegiance to the Church but they also found a strong cohesive in the undisturbed enjoyment of power. So long as de Gasperi remained in control the party's centrifugal tendencies were kept in check. De Gasperi stood head and shoulders above his contemporaries as one of the most gifted statesmen Italy has ever produced. His handling of home politics was in many ways as brilliant as Giolitti's (though its long-term consequences are more questionable) while in foreign affairs he showed diplomatic skill and moral stature on a level with Cavour. In 1945-6 he kept the party as little involved as possible in the controversy over the monarchy and the invidious question of the fascist purge and by so doing gained the confidence of the Allies and drew millions of frightened people to the catholic side; but he was never a popular figure in the country or even with his own party, nor was he loved in the Vatican. He was an austere and dedicated man, indifferent to his public image and lacking personal charm but steadfast, as few Italians have been, in his pursuit of what he believed to be the national, as distinct from class or party, interest. A greater contrast with Mussolini could hardly be found. He was born at Trento under Habsburg rule and his contemporaries sometimes found his style and culture more Germanic than Italian. They were perhaps more European. De Gasperi loved his native valleys but he was not marked with the indelible provincial stamp that most Italians bear. From 1929 to 1943 he lived as a political exile in the Vatican City, directing his attention to studying the political prospects for catholics in Europe. He saw the Socialist parties weakened by internal conflicts and thought the catholics could carve a place for themselves in the Centre, as heirs of both the socialists and the liberals. To do this they would have to take the welfare programme of the socialists and combine it with the constitutional principles of the liberals and, above all, they would have to resist the temptation to set up authoritarian integrationalist régimes. He admired the Belgian catholics who had governed their country on these lines, and he believed that, if the experiment were to succeed in Italy, it would have to be in co-operation with other constitutional parties. He dreaded a revival of religious intolerance, which he believed would certainly follow if the catholics ever tried to govern Italy alone. This, he thought, would necessarily provoke a coalition of the anticlerical parties, which must either lead to a Popular Front régime or a Spanish type of clerical fascism. Unlike most catholics on the Continent de Gasperi admired the Anglo-Saxon traditions of religious tolerance and humanitarian socialism and he thought that Europeans had much to learn from the British Labour party and from Roosevelt's New Deal.

Such ideas could scarcely be endorsed by the Vatican, at least while Pius XII was pontiff, but there was never any question of the Holy See vetoing de Gasperi's leadership of the Christian Democrats. Unlike its predecessor this party enjoyed the full backing of the Church. Many changes had occurred in the Vatican's attitude to Italian affairs since Pius XI signed the Lateran Treaties in 1929. The notion that fascist policies coincided with the interests of the catholic Church had become difficult to sustain in the late 1930's when Mussolini gave up his attempt to champion the small countries of Central Europe against Germany. Hitler's annexation of catholic Austria and his invasion of catholic Poland were severe blows to Vatican prestige and probably influenced the Church's belated revulsion against Nazi-fascist ideology. It is thought that Pius XI intended to mark the tenth anniversary of the Lateran Pacts by denouncing the abominations of racialism and pagan nationalism, but he fell ill that week and died. The attitude of his successor, Pius XII, to these matters is still the subject of historical controversy.

The collapse of the fascist régime and the ignominious flight of the King and his government allowed the Pope to stand forward as the only authority in Italy that had not abandoned its post. In the midst of chaos Italians found the Church taking over almost as she had done in the Dark Ages. The Pope's popularity in Rome soared. On the very day of the King's flight an air raid caused havoc to the popular quarter of San Lorenzo. Immediately the Pope was on the spot. What succour the city's population received during the dreadful months of German occupation came from the Vatican. Its doors, and those of various convents, were opened to political fugitives of every hue and many Jews who managed to escape from the Germans found refuge with the Church (though it seems that on the night the Germans raided the Ghetto, the gates of Vatican City remained closed). When the belligerents decided to consider Rome an open city no one doubted it was out of regard for the Pope, and the gratitude of the Romans to their bishop overflowed. Up in Salò Mussolini muttered that open city and Papal city were the same thing. He thought his handiwork had been undone and half expected Pius XII to denounce the Lateran Treaties and restore the temporal power, which shows how little he understood the Church.

When 'the man sent by Providence' was reduced to a puppet of the Germans, the Vatican shunned him and local bishops gave him only the barest *de facto* recognition. Their position in the north had become very strong as the result of the complicated struggle for power between Germans and fascists and between the Allies and the Resistance. In this fearful confusion the bishops stood firm, negotiating with all and sundry to save or succour the population and often playing a full-scale diplomatic role. In many places the local clergy opted for the Resistance and gave invaluable help to the partisans, whose roll of honour includes the names of many parish priests. In Milan the Archbishop's palace became the centre of top-level negotiations, and it was there that Mussolini had his last encounter with representatives of the CLNAI, the partisan forces of the north. While they were waiting in the Archbishop's study, a curious conversation took place between the aged prelate and the dictator on the run. Cardinal Schuster, who had once praised Mussolini as a new Constantine, was disconcerted to find that the man the Church had so exalted lacked the rudiments of catholic instruction.

Thanks to these events, at the end of hostilities the catholic Church in Italy was more popular and more powerful than she had been at any time since the unification. Her influence, wealth and experience were mobilized to support a political party of her choice. Never had the Popular party enjoyed the powerful backing the Church was ready to give the Christian Democrats, the only mass party that could hold its own against the communists and socialists. De Gasperi's problem was how to use this support without being overwhelmed by it. Local elections were held in Italy in May 1946, followed by the election of the Constituent Assembly in June. In both contests the Christian Democrats emerged as the biggest single party in the country though not quite so big as the combined socialist and communist Left. In the Assembly the Christian Democrats had 207 seats out of 555 for 8 million votes. The socialists followed with 115 seats and the communists with 104. Together the Left polled 9 million votes and for the first and only time in their postwar history the socialists outdid the communists by some 400,000 votes.

To observers it looked as though the initiative still rested with the Left. Together the socialists and communists controlled about half the administrative councils in the north and centre, including some of the major towns. In the Assembly they mustered close on half the votes and their leaders – Togliatti, di Vittorio, Nenni, Morandi – were names to conjure with among the workers and even with the peasants in the south. But there were inherent weaknesses in both parties and behind their reaffirmed political alliance there was not in fact a solidly united front. The major weakness lay in the contradiction between the revolutionary ideology both parties professed and the reality of Italy's position in Europe on the 'wrong' side of the Iron Curtain, which was inexorably falling even though, in 1946, it had not quite clanked down.

Togliatti alone faced up to the situation, coldly adapting his strategy to the circumstances. He was as brilliant a politician as de Gasperi, at grips with a similar problem: how to do the best for his party without pandering to its passions. What he feared was a false step which would get the Communist party outlawed (as the Americans were urging de Gasperi). He wished above all to avoid a situation like the one in Greece. He therefore sought to keep the PCI in government as long as possible in order to extend and consolidate its influence through government patronage without becoming involved in responsibility for the conduct of affairs. Since his purpose was the long-term conquest of power by constitutional means he needed a broad open party, not a tight revolutionary group; but he could never explain his strategy to the workers nor even to his own lieutenants in those days of messianic expectation of a new social order immediately after the war. His 'system' broke down in May 1947, when de Gasperi dropped the communists out of the government a few days after they had voted in favour of the incorporation of the Lateran Treaties in the Constitution. Exactly why Togliatti did this has never been satisfactorily explained. Article Seven, which would never have been passed without the communist vote, strengthened the power of the hierarchy and weakened the defences of the state. Perhaps that is what Togliatti desired.

The constitution voted in December 1947, after eighteen months' discussion in the Assembly, is a curious mixture of moral precepts, directives for government and declarations of intent. Its makers meant it to be rigid and to leave nothing to chance, but in fact it lacks clarity and precision and is so full of contradictions that some of its most important injunctions have been successfully evaded for over two decades. The constitution enjoins that Italy be divided into twenty-four semi-autonomous regions (like the Austrian *Länder*) but it did not actually create these regions, while it left the organs of centralized government and the prefectorial system intact. Four special regions were set up at once to combat local separatism in Sicily, Sardinia, Val d'Aosta and the Alto Adige. A fifth region, Friuli–Venezia Giulia, was set up much later (1963) when the controversy over Trieste had subsided; but the nineteen ordinary regions still await implementation, which has been promised again and again.[3]

Regional decentralization was one of the original tenets of Christian Democracy. The radical and marxist Left, which was strongly represented in the Constituent Assembly, also favoured the regional system as a means of fighting the old bureaucracy and eliminating the prefects. The catholics changed their attitude after the general election of 1948, when they found that while they had an over-all majority in the country, in central Italy they were weaker than the united communist and socialist Left. Interest in the regions revived in the early sixties in connection with the idea of economic planning, and in a new political context in which the socialists had broken their alliance with the communists to join a coalition of the Centre-Left. Even so the idea of decentralizing government still encountered prejudice and fear and its opponents pointed to the example of Sicily, where regional autonomy has hardly been identified with efficient and honest administration.

The Italian constitution endorses the classical separation of powers between the legislature, the executive and the magistracy. Parliament consists of two elected Chambers (though a number of senators are appointed for life) with similar powers and duration (five years). The President of the Republic is elected for seven years and is not responsible to Parliament but can be impeached before the Constitutional Court. He chooses the prime minister who then picks his own team but each minister is named by the President. This clause has given rise to discussion about the President's right to interfere in the formation of ministries, but in practice the prime minister's freedom is more curtailed by interference from the party secretaries than from the President of the Republic.

The constitution guarantees the usual civil rights but assumes that economic and social barriers may prevent the citizens from enjoying the equality allegedly offered them by the law. Hence a number of social clauses prescribing the right to work, to set up trade unions and to strike. Italy, says the constitution, is a republic founded upon labour. Private property and private enterprise are protected only in so far as they do not interfere with public utility, and the state has the right to expropriate and to plan.

Many of these tenets were too advanced for the society to which they applied and the constitution is more often appealed to by the opposition than by government. Ten years after its approval one of its makers ruefully observed that it had become a subversive document but now, in its third decade, Italians are beginning to catch up with it. This is partly due to the work of the Constitutional Court which was set up in 1955 (after eight years of hesitation) with the task of deciding when the law conflicts with the spirit of the constitution. Appeals to the Court are frequent and many laws have been attainted – a Court sentence does not automatically revoke the law – but Italians are still using the penal and civil codes and the procedure codes adopted during the dictatorship, although the need to revise them is deeply felt.

While the Constituent Assembly was sitting (June 1946–December 1947) a series of political crises marked the transition from the influence of the Resistance and the liberation committees to government by the Christian Democrats and the Centre-Right. De Gasperi's second government (July 1946 – February 1947) still included socialists and communists but in January 1947 the Socialist party split. The bulk of the party, led by Nenni, still looked on the Soviet Union as the natural leader of the workers' movement and stuck to its alliance with the PCI, but a minority hived off with Giuseppe Saragat to form a Social Democratic party. The schism was welcomed abroad and encouraged by the American labour unions as well as by the British Labour party[4] and the Social Democratic party of West Germany. Thanks to this support Saragat's party was recognized as the sole representative of Italian socialism in the Socialist International. For a long time both socialist parties in Italy were financially as well as ideologically bound to their respective international allies, and less than a year after the schism Saragat brought his party into government in a coalition of the Centre-Right.

9   Italy faces West

DE GASPERI'S CRITICS say he turned Italy into a satellite of the United States and blame him for the failure to get rid of a corrupt and reactionary Establishment. The charges are related, for it was largely to reassure the Americans in 1946 that he restored the career prefects and quashed the antifascist purge; as it was partly to satisfy the Americans that he dropped the communists from his government in 1947, though he would never accede to the American request to outlaw the PCI. De Gasperi was foreign minister and later prime minister during the peace talks of 1945–7 and, as such, his task was to steer Italy back to a place of consideration and reasonable influence among the western powers. His main difficulty came from the British government and Parliament, who not only wanted to strip Italy of her colonies, but tended to sympathize with the Austrian and Yugoslav claims against the Italian frontiers of 1919. De Gasperi had no choice but to turn for moral support to the United States, whose ministers, James Byrnes and Dean Acheson, showed sympathy for the Italian cause, as well as personal esteem for Italy's spokesman during the peace talks when all other delegates were as cold to de Gasperi as if he had been Mussolini in person.

All the nations that had been attacked by fascist Italy had territorial, financial or colonial accounts to settle with the Italian Republic. Against the claims put forward by Britain, France, Yugoslavia, Greece, Albania, Russia and Ethiopia (as well as by Austria whom the Allies chose to consider a 'liberated' country) Italy had no cards but the good will of the United States and the Latin American republics (Brazil in particular) and the Western Allies' fear of repeating the mistakes of Versailles, at least as regards reparations. The gravest frontier claim came from Yugoslavia, who demanded the whole of Venezia Giulia including Trieste. The town had been occupied by Tito's partisans in May 1945 but in June the Western Allies persuaded them to withdraw to a line which left Trieste and Pola in Anglo-American hands. In 1946 the Council of Foreign Ministers appointed a boundary commission which, being a four-power committee, produced four different solutions, and the Ministers eventually agreed on the French line, the least favourable to Italy after the Russian. This became the eastern boundary of the so-called Free Territory of Trieste, which was divided into zones A and B. Zone A included the city and remained under Anglo-American occupation. Zone B was occupied by Yugoslavia. Istria and the adjacent islands, with Fiume, Pola and Zara, were lost to Italy for ever. The occupation of Zones A and B was to be temporary until the United Nations Security Council appointed a neutral governor, but the Council could not agree and the boundary between the two zones became the *de facto* frontier between Italy and Yugoslavia.

In March 1948, after the Communist coup in Prague and just before the general election in Italy, the three Western Allies took fright at the idea of Trieste becoming a communist port in the Mediterranean and issued a proclamation saying that the whole of the Free Territory should be returned to Italy. But in July Tito fell out with Moscow and the Allies forgot their promise. In October 1953 Britain and the U.S. proposed making the division between Zones A and B permanent but Italy and Yugoslavia reacted sharply. Tito mobilized his troops near the frontier and the Italian premier Giuseppe Pella, who for reasons of domestic politics was courting the nationalist Right, sent Italian troops to Gorizia. However, the incident blew over without hurt, except in Trieste where a number of people were killed in scuffles with the British police. A year later the British handed over the administration of Zone A to Italy. Today Trieste is an integral part of the national territory, as it has been since 1918, but nostalgia for Istria and the lost Dalmatian cities is fading. Italy's experience in Greece and Yugoslavia in World War II put an end to the Adriatic yearnings fostered by D'Annunzio. Slowly and cautiously Italo-Yugoslav relations improved.

Another dispute concerned the Austrian request for the return of South Tyrol, that is the predominantly German-speaking province of Bolzano which Italy had acquired, together with the almost wholly Italian province of Trentino, in 1919. Later Mussolini tried to Italianize the region by encouraging the steel industry and importing Italian labour but, outside the town of Bolzano itself, the population remained overwhelmingly German. In 1939, after the annexation of Austria by the Third Reich, Hitler and Mussolini agreed to hold a plebiscite inviting the inhabitants to opt for Italy or the Reich. About two-thirds of the voters agreed to transfer to Germany and over 75,000 people had actually gone there when the situation was reversed by the Italian surrender of September 1943. Hitler annexed the region and many of the optants returned, some to join the Nazi administration of northern Italy.

The Italians based their claim to hang on to the Alto Adige, as they have always called the South Tyrol, on the fact that for part of the war they had been co-belligerents of the Allies whereas the Austrians had fought against them to the end. One hundred and fifty members of the British Parliament petitioned the Council of Ministers to return the South Tyrol to Austria but the powers decided in favour of Italy, doubtless to compensate her for the sacrifices she was required to make elsewhere. France and Britain, as well as Yugoslavia, were pressing their claims to Italian territory and colonies, and Austria, not being a victorious power, was in no position to compete. Italy was allowed to keep her 1919 frontier on the Brenner but she was invited to negotiate a bilateral agreement with Austria to safeguard the ethnic rights of the German population of South Tyrol. The de Gasperi-Gruber accord was signed in Paris in September 1946 but its wording was ambiguous and disputes arose about its application. Italy set up a self-governing region of the Alto Adige comprising the two provinces of Bolzano and Trentino, which correspond to the old Austrian administrative unit of South Tyrol. The arrangement leaves the Italian population predominant whereas the German-speaking inhabitants demand regional autonomy for Bolzano province alone. This has not been granted but lately the powers conceded to Bolzano have been increased. Anti-Italian feeling is still lively in the area, where a group of extremists have made terrorism endemic. It is thought that they are backed by neo-Nazi organizations in West Germany. Italians outside the area are not deeply interested, but should pan-Germanism again become a first-class international issue, emotional involvement in the Alto Adige could revive.

Italy and France resumed diplomatic relations in February 1945 but in April de Gaulle sent troops to occupy the French-speaking Val d'Aosta and adjacent territory in Piedmont. Under pressure from the British, and threats from President Truman, he withdrew and the Italian government promptly conceded regional autonomy to the Valdostani. France waived her claims but insisted on boundary rectifications in the Maritime Alps which gave her control of hydro-electric installations serving the cities of Genoa and Turin. The seizure of Briga and Tenda made a painful impression in Italy, where the Resistance had created the premise for a special relationship with France.[1] The incident rankled, but the trend in both countries, encouraged by de Gasperi, Sforza and Schuman, was towards a new type of European solidarity in which a major role was assigned to friendship between Italy and France.

No colonial power in 1945-6 foresaw the imminent liquidation of overseas empires, and Italy tried desperately to hang on at least to its pre-fascist colonies of Eritrea, Libya and Somaliland. British opposition was adamant, particularly as regards Libya. The Russians and Americans disliked colonial empires on principle and could not help. Only France supported Italy's colonial claims but the Allies could not agree on what to do with Italy's colonies except to take them from her. Eventually the United Nations gave Eritrea to Ethiopia. Libya became independent under British sponsorship, and Somaliland was granted to Italy as a United Nations trusteeship for ten years. The Italians soon discovered that they were well out of the imperial debacle and began to claim a special relationship with the under-developed countries as the only ex-colonial power with 'clean hands'.

The financial clauses of the Treaty were relatively mild. The U.S., Britain and France renounced their claims to reparations; but Italy had to pay Russia and the other claimants some 360 million dollars.

This was largely offset by American loans but the Italians felt they had already 'paid' for the war through the inflation caused by the circulation of Allied military lire.

Italians found the disarmament clauses humiliating, particularly the decision to confiscate the Navy which had not surrendered but joined the Allies voluntarily. Italy was required to dismantle her fortifications and forbidden to set up military installations on the Adriatic coast. Sicily and Sardinia were to be unfortified. Her armed forces were reduced to a minimum and she was forbidden to build or acquire battleships, submarines or bombers. De Gasperi told the Peace Conference that the Treaty left Italy defenceless but he was more embarrassed than reassured when the U.S. ambassador told him the Truman doctrine for the defence of Greece and Turkey was to be extended to Italy. When the Treaty was signed on 10 February 1947 President Truman warned that the U.S. were not indifferent to Italian security.

The antifascists in the Constituent Assembly were outraged by the Treaty which, they said, ignored their contribution to the Allied victory and went back on the promise that the Italian people would not be held responsible for the misdeeds of the dictator. But the government was told that American aid would cease if Italy failed to ratify the Treaty. In July 1947 Italy was invited to take part in the conference on the Marshall plan for the distribution of American aid to Europe. With this in view, as well as the desire to put an end to the military occupation, the Assembly authorized the government to ratify, in spite of the protests from such old liberals as Nitti, Orlando and Croce.

In spite of the outcry in the Assembly people were dimly aware that the Treaty was already obsolete. It was a sop to anti-Italian prejudice and rancour in Britain, France and Russia but it did not reflect the reality of Italy's international position at the end of 1947. This had improved since the peace talks began in 1945 and was to improve still further in the next two years until Italy became a member of Nato.

Until the Peace Treaty was signed and ratified de Gasperi tried to keep Italy uninvolved in the Cold War. He wanted to see her admitted to the United Nations and dared not antagonize any of the victors. Neither he nor his foreign minister, Count Sforza, was enthusiastic about joining the Atlantic alliance. Sforza seems to have hoped that Italy and France, who had signed a customs union in March 1948, could become the nucleus of a European Third Force to hold the balance between East and West. De Gasperi feared to exasperate the communists and socialists at home at a time when social conflict was endemic. Moreover he felt that public opinion would not understand involvement in a military alliance after Italy had been so drastically disarmed (for this reason he had refrained from asking to join the Brussels Pact in April 1948). But he was sincerely attracted to the idea of European union, the more so because, in a greater Europe, the handicaps inflicted on a defeated and discredited Italy would tend to disappear. His European ideals were shared by leading statesmen in France and Belgium (as well as Germany) and it was largely thanks to the personal influence of Robert Schuman and Paul-Henri Spaak, added to pressures from the United States, that de Gasperi brought Italy into such European organizations as OEEC and the Council of Europe, and at last took the plunge into Nato.

Perhaps without knowing it, Italy had made her choice for the West when she decided to accept Marshall Aid. In American eyes the European Recovery Programme was designed to combat communism through prosperity. Its announcement in July 1947 precipitated the great cleavage in Europe, for the Russians responded by calling the conference of European Communist parties at Bialystok which set up the Cominform, and enjoined the Poles and Czechs to refuse Marshall Aid. These events, followed by the Communist coup d'état in Prague, had a bearing on the Italian general election of April 1948, the first to be held since fascism. Pressures from the Vatican and the U.S. turned the election into an anti-communist crusade in which a Popular Front formation of socialists and communists faced the Christian Democrats while the lesser parties were over-shadowed. As a result de Gasperi's Christian Democrats obtained an absolute majority in the Chamber with 307 seats to 182 for the Left.

The victory sanctioned Italy's alignment with the West; but neither the Vatican nor the Catholic party as a whole was ready to translate this into commitment to a military alliance dominated by the protestant powers. When de Gasperi finally made up his mind to join Nato he had to take Count Sforza with him personally to convince the Pope. The ultimate argument, incessantly pressed by his ambassador in Washington, Tarchiani, was that United States aid would cease if Italy kept aloof. At the last de Gasperi was influenced by American assurance that, while no Italian conditions for joining Nato could be accepted, the question of Italy's rearmament would be examined in a new spirit once she had joined.

American pressure to bring Italy into Nato was a proof of United States interest in the Mediterranean sector and explains the coolness shown by the British government towards Italian participation. Ernest Bevin, the British socialist foreign minister, objected that Italy was too weak militarily to pull her weight in the alliance which, he claimed, ought to be strictly limited to the Atlantic area. Though shared by the Canadians and the Norwegians, this objection was overcome and for the next twenty years, in spite of vociferous opposition at home from communists and socialists, Italy was to be the most docile and compliant of America's partners in Nato. Italian delegates at international meetings had standing orders to 'vote with the Americans'.

10   Right Centre, Left Centre

THROUGHOUT THE FIRST PARLIAMENT (1948–53) de Gasperi headed a series of governments based on a coalition of Christian democrats, liberals, republicans and social democrats. The smaller parties were not in government the whole time but they almost always formed part of its majority. This was perpetually torn between its conservatives and progressives, with the right-wingers pulling a good deal harder than the Left. The coalition took over at a time of violent social unrest. Inflation and unemployment, following on the tremendous dislocations of the war, were the background to incessant strikes and demonstrations, encouraged by the communists, and to peasant marches and squattings on the big, under-cultivated estates. In Calabria, Apulia and the Roman Campagna, as in Sicily and Sardinia, the people were demanding land. Social tension reached a peak during the general strike which followed the attempt on Togliatti's life in July 1948. But the most tragic episode occurred in Sicily in 1950 when Giuliano and his band of outlaws, to whom certain influential Sicilians had promised rewards and immunity, machine-gunned a group of peasants at a communist May Day celebration. The massacre at Pian dei Giullari was the most outrageous, though by no means the last attempt in Sicily to stop reform by means of terrorism.

Since 1947 United States influence was paramount in Italy and the American administrators of Marshall Aid pressed the government to undertake substantial reforms. Under the Truman administration the officials in charge of the European Recovery Programme were still imbued with the spirit of the New Deal. They wanted Italy to fight communism through prosperity, and urged the introduction of a more enlightened tax system and other measures tending to

137

promote a more equitable distribution of wealth. Their ideas were alien to the mentality of the Italian business world, which expected governments to provide industry with protection from foreign competitors while allowing it complete freedom of action at home.

Thanks partly to these pressures as well as to the genuine zeal of the more enlightened part of its majority, the government embarked on a land-reform scheme for which it originally earmarked some three and a half million acres to be carved out of the under-cultivated estates. The owners were to receive cash compensation. Opposition to the scheme was so fierce that it stalled for three years and was finally whittled down to one-third. In 1950 a law was passed for the redistribution of land in Calabria and another for the Po Delta, Maremma and Sardinia. Land reform in Sicily was left to the regional government. Technically the reform was ill-conceived. The land given to the peasants was poor and the holdings were often too small to be viable while the education and training necessary for the development of an independent co-operative system was lacking. The agencies set up to assign the land, provide stock and give technical advice became instruments of Christian Democrat patronage but by and large the reform failed of its political purpose, which was to create a class of small farmers devoted to government and to Christian democracy. Less than one in fifty of Italy's six million landless peasants received a farm, so that more people were disappointed than pleased. Southern landowners were irritated and gave their votes to the Right while the peasants slowly transferred their support from the monarchists to the communists. None the less, thanks to large investments in irrigation and reclaiming, a good deal of new land was brought under cultivation (some of it has been abandoned since) and the countryside was cleared of the scourge of malaria, a fact of incalculable importance which has altered the lives of millions of Italians.

In 1950 the government set up the Cassa per il Mezzogiorno, a large fund and administration for the development of the south. Its original endowment was £60 million a year for ten years but this has been increased and prolonged many times. The Cassa's first task was to improve the conditions for agriculture and secondly to create incentives to attract industry. Its early activity was mainly devoted to building dams and aqueducts and other works connected with land-reclaiming, and through its agencies it soon became the most important source of patronage in the south. Italians have always looked on patronage as the sinews of power. The Christian Democrats, with their virtual monopoly of the land-reform agencies and the Cassa, disposed of a network of jobs, contracts, permits, credits and other favours such as no Italian government had ever enjoyed. The entire economy, immediately after the war, was geared to a programme of public works to provide employment, repair war damage and supply housing for the rapidly swelling population of the towns. Rarely, in Italy, had there been such a frenzy of speculation in real estate, such shoving and pushing to obtain government contracts, building permits and the like. No previous boom had offered similar opportunities for corruption and graft. This was no longer the calculated political corruption practised by Giolitti for a broader political end. It was a stampede, a free-for-all, in which the politicians jostled each other to grab the patronage that would reward their clients, enrich their families and friends, and strengthen the influence of factions and individuals. All the political parties joined the scramble but the Christian Democrats had such an advantage that there was little left for their allies but the crumbs. De Gasperi, with catholic acceptance of the frailty of human nature, turned his head the other way. His sights were glued to the international horizon. But he was as much responsible for the lowering of the moral tone of politics after 1947 as Giolitti had been in his day. Giolitti met his Cato in Salvemini. Ernesto Rossi, Salvemini's disciple, became the chastiser of the vices of this later age.[1]

Unemployment was Italy's biggest problem in the first decade after the war. Some two million workers, a tenth of the labour force, were jobless, and probably as many more were under-employed. As late as 1955 agriculture still occupied 40 per cent of the labour force while the service industries, which took in the greater part of the exodus from the farms, were crowded with small-time craftsmen and retailers, some of them little more than peddlers. Distribution was splintered into a myriad small units and over-loaded with middlemen, whose function was not always distinguishable from the blackmailing activities of the Mafia and the Camorra in the south. In 1952 Parliament ordered two inquiries into poverty and unemployment. The results filled twenty volumes and were hardly accessible to the public, whose attitude remained uninformed.

Unemployment was not new in Italy. The traditional answer to it was to lay on public works and leave the rest to emigration. Italian industry, snugly fitted into the protective shell it had built for itself before and during fascism, had found little stimulus to expand. Its policy was to secure as large a slice as possible of a small domestic pie, and in the difficult years after World War I it had succeeded in handing over its worst headaches to the state. The philosophy of free enterprise so passionately professed by the Italian business world had been shared by governments and although railways were nationalized in 1905 and a few industries of national importance – steel and shipyards for instance – received subsidies and other forms of protection, it was only with the economic crisis of the early twenties that Italy started an original form of state intervention which consisted in the government acquiring the controlling stock interest in certain industrial firms. The real purpose of the operation was to salvage the banks, which had over-reached themselves in loans to heavy industry during the war. Thus in 1921–22 the Ilva steel works and Ansaldo shipyards passed to the state and a special institute, IMI (Istituto Mobiliare Italiano), was set up to handle long-term industrial loans. Ten years later it again became necessary to bail out industries and banks caught up in the great depression, and in 1933 the fascist government set up the Institute for Industrial Reconstruction (IRI), whose task was to regroup and co-ordinate the enterprises that had come into the possession of the state. Some of these were sold back to private ownership once they were on their feet, but when Mussolini intensified his autarkic wartime policy IRI was made a permanent institution for financing industry, and the major banks – all banks had been forbidden to make loans to industry – passed under IRI's control. IRI and IMI were potential instruments for a government-directed investment policy but the confusion of the times, and the mystique of private enterprise, prevented them from being used.

At the end of World War II IRI had activities in ten fields with a predominant interest in shipyards and steel, two sectors which had been sorely hit by the war and were handicapped by the peace treaty limitations on Italian armaments. They were also desperately over-manned. IRI's labour force had doubled during the war while its productive capacity was halved. When peace came there was no over-all plan of reconstruction for the public sector and the only government directive was to keep the men on the pay rolls. Each IRI group tried to build up to its pre-war capacity and the shipyards were restored to their wartime strength regardless of the fact that the demand for tonnage had shrunk. The same criterion was applied to the railways. The shift to road transport was not foreseen. Thus handicapped, and given its pre-war history, IRI did not seem the best instrument for a policy of planned expansion. The Constituent Assembly, with its strong socialist bias, had been in favour of 'socializing' (a euphemism for nationalizing) certain industries but discarded the idea of using IRI for the purpose. State participation in industry continued to be disorderly and scattered and in 1951 it proved difficult even to make a complete list of IRI's interests.[2]

None the less IRI was to play a big part in Italy's industrial recovery when the time came, thanks to the presence of the right man. In 1952, when Italy joined the Coal and Steel Community, Oscar Sinigaglia was in charge of IRI's steel group. Italy entered the Community at a disadvantage. Her coal was scarce and poor and her steel industry had always needed protection. She was granted five years' grace to bring it up to the European level and such was the energy and talent of Sinigaglia that she succeeded. In 1957 Italy entered the Common Market with a steel industry as efficient and competitive as any in Europe.

Meanwhile, under the stimulus of new contacts, the opening of frontiers and the 'European' ethos of the times, the business world began to raise its sights. In 1949 the government abolished import quotas and the newest models of foreign machinery and equipment began to flow in. The great programme of public works for the south set up a demand for machinery and capital goods from the north and became one of the most decisive factors in Italy's industrial take-off. In ten years, it was calculated, the south ran up a £500 million deficit in its 'balance of payments' with the north. Italian labour was still cheap by European standards and this too was a stimulus to growth. Italy started her second industrial revolution by producing capital goods for the government and for export. The spread to consumer goods came when Italian wages leapt up between 1962 and 1964.

Modernization plus cheap labour and an expanding European market all contributed to Italy's industrial renaissance, but there was another important element: the discovery of natural gas in the Po Valley, and the uses to which this was put by the extraordinary Enrico Mattei. The reserves were located in 1945 and in a short time Mattei had turned the old state prospecting company AGIP, which he had been instructed to wind up, into the cornerstone of a personal hydrocarbon empire from whose throne he dominated Italian politics for nine years and challenged the international oil world. ENI, the national hydrocarbon agency, was created in 1953 with a legal structure similar to that of IRI. It was a state holding company controlling a number of operating companies all theoretically connected with oil or natural gas and their derivatives. But whereas IRI had grown up as a salvaging institution for the comfort of the private sector, Mattei looked upon ENI as an instrument of aggression, whose purpose was to give life to a policy of economic expansion willed and directed, in theory, by the state. So long as Mattei was at ENI's helm it was he who did the willing and directing and his power to do this came from the profits that were rolling in from the natural gas he was selling to industry in the north. For in 1953, notwithstanding the opposition of the international oil companies and the pressure exerted on their behalf by the United States ambassador Mrs Clare Booth Luce, ENI was given the monopoly of hydrocarbon prospecting and development in the Po Valley.

The gas reserves were large and the profits immense, for the price of gas was tied to that of electricity and coal, so that ENI, which had received an initial endowment of £18 million, soon became self-financing and was therefore in great measure independent of the state. In fact it disposed of 'secret funds' which enabled Mattei to manipulate the political parties and factions in order to obtain the political covering for his policies. Basically he had the same realistic, or pessimistic, approach to Italian politics as Giolitti and de Gasperi and, like Giolitti, he was ready to use corruption more or less openly for what he considered a noble and superior end. The passion that moved him was the desire to see Italy's industrial standing improve and, with it, the status of Italian workers at home and abroad. It was a crusade against the humiliations of poverty which he had suffered personally in his youth. Chance gave him the control of an important source of energy and he was hell bent to use this both directly and indirectly to change the structure of the Italian economy and give it new life.

To do this he had to fight the taboos and privileges of the business community, whose restrictive mentality and anti-southern prejudice were a check on the nation's growth. The clash was violent and stimulating, for each side controlled or had allies in important sections of the press. Mattei was a catholic; he had led the catholic Partisan formations during the Resistance, and his chief political instrument was the Christian Democrat party, or more precisely those factions in the party which either thought as he did or could be brought over to his views. To laissez-faire liberals and the Italian Confederation of Industries he was a scourge of God, but since the private 'monopolies' had singled him out as their enemy, the socialists and communists were his natural allies, while the radical supporters of a planned economy necessarily rallied to his side.

In all probability the war between the public and private sectors, which was waged with such passion during Mattei's life-time, was salutary and helped Italy to expand. ENI did not have as big a share of the chemical and petrochemical industries as IRI had of steel, and the rivalry between Mattei's group and the big private companies – Montecatini and Edison in particular, but also the Italian affiliations of Esso and Shell – was a factor in the development of the south. The big petrochemical installations at Gela (ENI) and Brindisi (Montecatini, later Montecatini-Edison) were born of this dispute. Moreover, Mattei's example affected IRI, giving the government the courage to use it in a more effective way. But for the precedents created by

Mattei, it is unlikely that either the government or IRI itself would have found the strength to overcome the 'ideological' difficulties which were raised to prevent the building of the great IRI steel plant in Taranto. In theory, it is true, industrial investments by ENI and IRI in the south were the consequence of special legislation passed in 1957 after the creation of a special ministry for state shares. But the ministry itself has always been the handmaid rather than the mistress of ENI and all the theoretical planning that was being done in Italy in the late fifties would have been no more than an intellectual exercise without Mattei.

So long as the war between Mattei and private enterprise was confined to Italy, both sides understood the rules of the game. It became more brutal and dangerous when Mattei began to expand his empire abroad. The hostility of the international oil companies, who refused to admit him to their consortium in Iran, caused him to offer the Persian government a new type of oil contract on the basis of 75 per cent of the profits to the host country and 25 per cent to the company (in which the government of the host country would have a share). The agreement shattered the old fifty-fifty system which the oil companies had imposed for so long. Mattei built up an ideological and political mystique for his system, in which he sincerely believed, and which he soon extended to Egypt and Libya and thence to the developing countries formerly under British or French colonial rule. He was sustained in this by certain Christian Democrat leaders, notably Gronchi, Fanfani and La Pira, who shared his vision of Italy as the radiating centre of a new Mediterranean area of economic and cultural influence.

It was the old idea of Catholic penetration in Africa and among the Arabs, in the wake, this time, not of Italian arms but of Italian trade. It contained an unconfessed desire to get even with the British and the French, whose discomfiture at Suez, coupled to the humiliation of France in Algiers, seemed to offer the Italians an opportunity to become, if not the leading power in the Mediterranean, at least America's leading Mediterranean ally. Fanfani, who followed up Mattei's oil deal with Egypt by an official visit to Nasser, was the first Nato premier to accede to the United States' request for atomic medium-range anti-missile bases. The attempt to put Italy's Mediterranean vocation into practice helped Mattei to build up his oil empire but was otherwise politically sterile for it was based on a too simple approach to the complexities of Arab politics and post-colonial Africa.

The Centre Coalition (Christian Democrats, Liberals, Social Democrats and Republicans) continued to govern Italy throughout the second Parliament (1953–58) and most of the third (1958–63). The Christian Democrats lost the absolute majority in the Chamber, falling back to 40 per cent (42 per cent in 1958), while the factions, which flourished on the manipulation of patronage, grew more powerful and difficult to control. De Gasperi lost his grip of the party in 1953 when an unpopular election law, which was to have given the Centre parties a large bonus, actually caused them to lose votes. Fanfani became party secretary in 1954 and for a time was the outstanding figure in the party, but his fortunes waxed and waned with those of his vaguely Left-Centre faction, which lost its preponderance in 1959 to a coalition of moderates known as the Dorotheans (after a meeting in the convent of Saint Dorothy), who were determined that no one should ever again control the party as de Gasperi had done. Henceforth the Dorotheans, themselves divided into various cliques, were to be the dominant group among the Christian Democrats, and politics became more and more a matter of intrigue and negotiation between the factions, a sort of incessant molecular grouping and regrouping which absorbed all the political energy of the participants while it deprived the formal institutions of democracy – Parliament, the prime minister, the cabinet – of real power. The factions had their own offices and press sections and were the recipients of financial aid from pressure groups, national and foreign, whose interests they were ready to promote. In Parliament the party voted as the factions had agreed and ministers were looked on as the 'delegates' in government of their faction.

The only authority whose powers were relatively unimpaired by the system was the President of the Republic, which explains why the struggle to control the presidency became a main issue of politics as from the election of Gronchi in 1955. Though proper to the

Christian Democrats, the system spread to the other parties and was particularly harmful to the socialists, among whom it aggravated the innate tendency to split. The factions, it must be understood, are power groups. The ideological differences between them, if we except the extreme catholic (and socialist) Left, are almost nil.

The decade 1953–63 was characterized by the struggle put up by the conservative forces in Italy, particularly in the business world and in the Church, to resist modernizing reforms. Whenever possible the struggle was sublimated to the sphere of foreign politics and camouflaged as an ideological campaign against communism. The transposition was made easier by the trend of U.S. policies and pressures during the Eisenhower administration, under the influence of Foster Dulles. In Rome the U.S. ambassador, Mrs Luce, pressed the government to outlaw the communists and extend the coalition to the monarchists on the right. The government resisted these pressures, which were clumsy and naïve, but it took advantage of American encouragement to ignore the Peace Treaty injunction and build up the Italian navy and air force with U.S. aid. Off-shore orders to Italian industry, which undoubtedly played a part in Italy's industrial recovery, were manipulated at the instigation of Mrs Luce to put pressure on the Italian trade unions and weaken the communist-dominated CGIL. Firms in which the communist unions controlled fifty per cent of the workers' committees were to be excluded from U.S. orders, and in 1955 the CGIL lost its majority at Fiat.[3]

Whether the manoeuvre seriously weakened the unions is hard to say. The Italian labour movement had aready suffered from the trade-union splits of 1948–50 when the Christian democratic and social democratic labour leaders left the CGIL and set up federations of their own. This was in part a reaction to the excessive political exploitation of the CGIL by the communists, who were forcing the unions to call strikes against Marshall Aid and so forth. Vatican and American pressures helped the Christian democrats to set up their trade-union federation, CISL, which soon stood a good second to the still predominant CGIL. The Americans also helped the social democrats to set up their own smaller federation, UIL. Politically American 'persecutions' were more useful to the communists than the reverse. PCI leaders were as eager as the conservatives to transfer domestic conflicts to the sphere of foreign politics and cover up the weakness of their home policies (where they kept up a doctrinaire opposition to reforms) by crying out against Nato and rearmament.

One aspect of Right-Centre government closely connected with its anti-communist bias was the important role assigned to the police. Mario Scelba, a tough Sicilian lawyer, who was minister for internal affairs (1947–53) and afterwards prime minister (1954–55), carved his name in Italian history as the founder of a mobile police squad – the *Celere* (Swift) – specially trained and equipped to deal with political demonstrations, disperse strikers and so forth. The Celere soon earned the special enmity of workers and students and though later on an effort was made in the police schools to give trainees a democratic education, the police as a body were looked on as a hostile force and the potential instrument of right-wing intervention. This made the minister of internal affairs more than ever a key position in the elaborate power game of Italian politics.

Right wing pressure groups included the American Embassy, the Confederation of Industries, Catholic Action (later dominated by its own left), the Curia and the Christian democrat farmers' federation. This last was a rich and powerful consortium which handled large funds arising out of the administration of the wheat pools. Its leader, Paolo Bonomi, controlled about sixty deputies and could make life difficult for any government that tried to reduce the support price of wheat. The Coltivatori Diretti were in fact the only genuine lobby in Parliament apart from the never officially recognized ENI lobby controlled by Enrico Mattei.

Vatican interference in Italian politics became more blatant after de Gasperi's death in 1954. His successors found it harder to resist the pressures, vetoes and recommendations of the hierarchy, for not only the Christian Democrat party as a whole, but its factions, which were the real centres of power, depended on the good will of the clergy for the huge catholic vote which gave them control of the state. During the last years of Pius XII's pontificate Vatican politics were dominated by a reactionary group of cardinals of the Roman Curia among whom Cardinal Ottaviani, Secretary of the Holy Office, was the most outspoken. He was not averse to interfering directly in Italian politics but on the whole the Curia preferred the indirect method, which consisted in using the personal channels that had been so carefully prepared in order to influence the behaviour of Christian Democrat politicians on all matters of real concern to the Church. The time had come to pluck the fruits of the Concordat, whose incorporation in the constitution enabled the Church to claim a legal as well as a moral voice in matters concerning marriage, education, morals and the like. Most important to the Church was its influence upon education and its veto on the introduction of divorce but it was equally insistent on claiming exemption from a dividends tax which would damage the immense Vatican portfolio.

The rearguard action fought by Italian conservatives could not indefinitely stave off the social 'revolution' that was bound to follow the great economic changes sweeping the country. The purpose of this action was to maintain the legal structure of the old élite society in the hope that, so long as its laws were intact, that society could survive. Hence the delaying tactics employed to retard the revision of the fascist codes – penal, civil and procedural – and the resistance to any radical change of the tax system, still based preponderantly on indirect taxation. Hence too the opposition to the administrative decentralization enjoined by the constitution, and the passionate resistance to a reform of education which would alter a class structure based on the prestige of the classics. Finally the almost hysterical opposition to economic planning and the nationalization of the electric power industry stemmed from the same emotional hostility to change and the unconfessed aversion of Italian conservatives, both lay and clerical, to the development of the south. But the logic of economic change was inexorable. Between 1955 and 1958 Italy jumped the barrier between a rural and an industrial economy and by 1960 the Italian Miracle was in full swing. That year, which saw a supreme effort on the part of the conservatives to put the clock back, was also a political watershed.

The shift from a Right-Centre to a Left-Centre coalition was a slow and laborious process involving several false starts. The operation known as the Opening to the Left implied dropping the liberals out of the government majority and embarking the socialists. It also meant reconciling the social democrats to the loss of their privileged position for, in the final stage of the exercise, the two socialist parties, which had stood divided since 1947 and in bitter polemic under Nenni and Saragat, were to reunite. The Opening to the Left also spelt a more or less complete breach between the Nenni socialists and the communists. As early as 1953 Nenni, whose party fared poorly in the elections, decided to free the PSI from its subjection to the communists, but he was not able to do this until the great crisis of world communism following on the denunciation of Stalin and the rebellions in Poland and Hungary in 1956 destroyed the image of an ideal socialist society which he himself had helped to foster. To symbolize the rupture Nenni returned the Stalin prize he had been awarded a few years before. Not all the Socialists were ready to follow him in his new anti-Soviet line. The Carristi, apologists of the Russian armoured cars in Budapest, formed the nucleus of an opposition that was to leave the party when this finally joined a Left-Centre government in 1963.

Among the Christian Democrats the chief promoters of the Opening to the Left were Gronchi, who became President of the Republic with help from the socialists in April 1955, and Fanfani, who was party secretary from 1954 to 1959. Fanfani's government of 1958-9 was an experiment to see how far he could make the Christian Democrats follow him to the left. It failed because he made himself unpopular with the factions by trying to give the party a tightly organized apparatus of which he was to hold the strings. This was something the Christian Democrats would never tolerate. Fanfani was betrayed on a vote in the Chamber of 'sharp-shooters' from his own side, but he was also demoralized by the hostility of the Vatican and resigned the party secretaryship when his government fell. He was to return to the premiership two years later, a wiser man.

The reasons which ultimately compelled the Christian Democrats to seek an alliance with the socialists were rooted in their acceptance of the social changes attending economic growth. Unlike the liberals, who merely wanted to keep the clock back, the Christian Democrats were aware that their political domination depended on their ability to move with the times. Even the party's most conservative elements had no doctrinaire objections to planning and nationalization of industry. What they really feared as a possible consequence of an alliance with the socialists was a secularizing effect upon education and morals which could erode their influence and power. The same motive impelled the Curia to intervene again and again to prevent the final clinching of the alliance.

In the spring of 1960 these pressures led Italy into serious trouble. Twice the Church's veto inhibited the ex-premiers Segni and Fanfani from forming a Left-Centre coalition supported by the socialists, although the only alternative at this point was to fall back on a minority government dependent on the votes of the fascists. With ability and infinite patience Aldo Moro, who succeeded Fanfani as Christian Democrat party secretary in 1959, had persuaded the Dorotheans (who were now the dominant faction) to accept the Opening to the Left as a historical necessity, but before the Curia and the business world could also be convinced of this Italy had to experience the tumults and the barricades of June 1960. Given the impasse created by the Church, President Gronchi had somewhat inexplicably invited Fernando Tambroni, an ambitious demagogic character who, as minister of the interior, had collected dossiers on his cabinet colleagues, to form a 'non-political' interim government. Tambroni got by with 24 votes from the MSI, and the fascists, finding themselves politically indispensable for the first time since 1943, began to throw their weight about in the country and organized a national congress in Genoa, a city particularly associated with the Resistance. Italy was not in a mood to tolerate a revival of fascist insolence. The reaction was spontaneous and immediate, though later demonstrations were organized to some extent by the communists. There were riots in Genoa and Reggio Emilia and tumults in other cities, including Rome (where mounted police charged the crowd with unnecessary ferocity). In two weeks of tumult ten demonstrators were killed and many more wounded. Tambroni lost his head and accused his colleagues of conspiring against him. The government fell and the conservatives were finally convinced that no move to the right was possible without the risk of open conflict.

Two more years of patient negotiation were necessary before the Opening to the Left was at last achieved under the premiership of Fanfani, in its first preliminary phase, and finally under Moro, who was to remain prime minister from 1963 to 1968. Before this happened numerous local administrations, including the regional governments of Sicily and Val d' Aosta, experimented with the alliance – in some cases, as with Milazzo's freak government in Palermo, with the addition of the communists. Meanwhile the international context, always of supreme importance to domestic Italian politics, particularly in view of the influence of United States pressures, was changing radically since the advent of the Kennedy administration. To the dismay of Italian conservatives, East-West relations were thawing and the anti-communist crusade was no longer being preached by a Church that was moving towards the Oecumenical Council. After nearly two years of quiet preparation, Pope John emerged as a towering figure whose presence completely altered the familiar landscape of Italian catholicism.

Among the external factors which helped to determine the political swing to the left was a change of attitude of the British Labour party and the Socialist International towards Nenni, who at last succeeded in convincing western socialists of his sincere attachment to the method and theory of parliamentary democracy. Saragat's position as leader of the Italian social democrats had been entirely based on his American-sponsored anti-communist and anti-Soviet line. In the political climate of the late 1950's this was not enough to assure him the unconditional backing of western socialism and pressures began to be exerted from London and elsewhere to get the two Italian socialist parties to reunite.

11   The miracle fades

BETWEEN 1958 AND 1963 the Italian economy took on a spurt so
vigorous that it landed Italy among the first-class industrial powers.
Since World War II only West Germany and Japan could show a
similar record. The annual growth rate exceeded the five per cent
scheduled by the so-called Vanoni Plan of 1955 (one of the numerous
attempts to *plan* economic development which ended in a mere
schedule of projections and targets). Industrial output was making
great frog leaps of 10 per cent in 1959, 20.3 per cent in 1960, 13.7
and 13.4 per cent in 1961 and 1962. Italy's growth rate was the highest
of the six countries in the European Economic Community and her
foreign trade was expanding faster than that of any European
member of OECD. She was the first European country to import
Russian crude oil (one of Mattei's ventures to get even with the
international oil companies), but it was in Europe that her trade
expanded most. She had the highest increase of intra-EEC trade
among the Six.

   Her initial advantage in the European market came from cheap
labour. In his blunt way Enrico Mattei alleged that 'the Italian
Miracle rested on the backs of the poor.' Italy joined the Common
Market in response to her 'European Vocation' but also under pressure
from the business community, whose spokesman on this occasion
was the liberal foreign minister, Gaetano Martino, who promoted
the preliminary Common Market talks at Messina in 1956. But the
advantage of cheap labour did not last as long as Italian employers
had expected, for the expansion of the economy was so rapid, and
led to such an overwhelming afflux of population into the towns,
and to such a spasmodic demand for housing, that for the first time

in Italian history both skilled and unskilled labour were in short supply. Wages bounced up between 1962 and 1964 as the unions recovered their bargaining power, and such was the demand for skilled labour that many employers were offering more than the union rates. The result was a demand for consumer goods which sent prices up and made imports rocket. A revolutionary change in Italian eating habits occurred, with an unprecedented demand for meat. By 1964 wages were nearing the European level while meat imports were proving a major cause of balance of payments troubles. With a trade deficit of £500 million Italy was heading for a recession and by the time (December 1963) the four Left-Centre parties had at last got the coalition into gear the recession was in full swing.

The balance of payments deficit had been met by a conventional credit squeeze and other anti-inflationary measures, introduced at the instigation of the governor of the Bank of Italy by an interim government which had taken over while the four parties were negotiating their accords. These measures had the effect of discouraging investments and were hardly compatible with the ambitious economic development programme which was being elaborated in the new planning department set up by the first Left-Centre government in 1962.

One effect of the recession was to revive the hopes and combativity of the conservatives, who were by no means reconciled to the Centre-Left alignment. This had indeed got off to a very sticky start. Its only exploit was the nationalization of the electric power industry in October 1962. The first Left-Centre government, headed by Fanfani, fell after the general election of May 1963, at which the Christian Democrats lost some ground and the communists gained. The President of the Republic, Antonio Segni, whose election had been imposed by the Dorotheans as the price of their support for the Left-Centre, was not friendly to the alignment and his presence at the Quirinal strengthened the conservatives.

In spite of these difficulties, in December 1963, Aldo Moro became prime minister of a Centre-Left coalition which included the socialists, who were back in government for the first time since 1947 with Nenni as deputy prime minister. Not all the socialists liked this, and some twenty PSI deputies broke away to form an orthodox socialist party of their own, the PSIUP, whose orientation was vaguely Trotskyist, so that for a while there were three socialist parties in Italy, one in opposition (PSIUP) and two in government (Nenni's PSI and Saragat's PSDI which later united).[1] Inside Nenni's party a back-bench opposition headed by Riccardo Lombardi kept up a Cassandra-like hostility to the coalition. Lombardi thought the Dorotheans (one of whom, Rumor, had succeeded Moro as party secretary when the latter became prime minister) were not sincerely committed to the reforms that had been agreed on after extensive negotiation between the parties. He also thought the socialists could do no good and could only hurt themselves by accepting government responsibility at a time of economic crisis. The Governor of the Bank of Italy, Carli, and the minister of the Treasury, Colombo (another Dorothean), were pressing for a wage freeze and other anti-inflationary measures and the government was under pressure from the EEC executive to balance payments and drop the reforms. Capital was fleeing the country in an artificially created atmosphere of panic which was being whipped up on purpose to bring the Left-Centre coalition to grief. The economic and moral sabotage almost succeeded in the summer of 1964 when a government crisis made it necessary for the four parties to negotiate afresh.

It was Nenni who persuaded the socialists, against the advice of Lombardi, to go back into government, although the new accords were far from satisfying the party. Nenni was convinced that if they wasted any more time the conservatives would go to the length of staging a *coup d'état* in order to prevent a restoration of Left-Centre government. His fears seemed exaggerated at the time, although the conservative press was urging the President of the Republic to appoint a government *outside* the political parties and in Paris de Gaulle was crowing that Italy had reached 'the hour of the Fourth Republic'. But the events of July 1964 were seen in a new light three years later when it transpired that an emergency plan, or at least the embryo of such a plan, had actually existed.

General de Lorenzo, Commander of the Carabinieri Corps and a former chief of military counter-espionage (the organization known as SIFAR), had made provision for the arbitrary arrest and deportation of numerous political personalities whose names were given to a select group of Carabinieri officers. These were told to stand by for the order to proceed and were given to understand that the general was acting on personal instructions from the President of the Republic and without the knowledge of the ministers of defence and the interior. The whole truth about the SIFAR plot has still to be ascertained. In August 1964 President Segni was struck down by cerebral thrombosis and lost his faculties. De Lorenzo later won a libel suit against the newspaper *L'Espresso* which had published the story, but he was removed from the position of Commander-in-Chief of the Army to which he had been promoted in 1966. A parliamentary inquiry into the misuse of SIFAR funds and dossiers for political espionage and blackmail was eventually ordered after a great deal of hedging by the government behind the excuse of military secrets. The affair came to light at the time of the military *coup d'état* in Athens in 1967 and although most Italians discarded the possibility of a similar take-over in Italy, they had to admit that, if the political will for such action were forthcoming, the co-operation of the police and the military would not be hard to obtain.

The crisis passed in July 1964 and the new edition of the Left-Centre coalition soon proved so bland and moderate that the conservatives were reconciled to it. For the duration of the fourth Parliament (1963–68) not a single one of the so-called structural reforms touching regional government, the universities, the magistracy, the penal and civil codes, the health services, pensions and so forth, made any appreciable progress and the programme announced by the Left-Centre parties in December 1963 and reiterated in July 1964 was still to do when the coalition pulled itself together again for a third attempt in December 1968.

Italy snapped out of her recession more quickly than the experts anticipated, thanks in no small measure to a huge loan ($1,000m.) from the United States which helped to redress her balance of payments in 1964–5 and to reconcile Italian conservatives to a government which clearly enjoyed the good will of America. This checked the flight of Italian capital to Switzerland, but the credit squeeze and other anti-inflationary measures which the government was obliged to take had the effect of checking investments and so plunging Italy once more into her eternal dilemma: inflation or unemployment. The hope that structural unemployment could be eliminated by the early seventies vanished and a new appraisal of economic policy became necessary as the social problems created by the boom and its aftermath became more serious and pressing.

The Miracle had served to accelerate the biggest internal migration in Italian history. In twelve to fifteen years some three and a half million people had moved away from their homes, sometimes abandoning them completely. The shocking waste of the land reform of the early fifties was revealed as people came away from their arid little farms. In Central Italy whole villages on the Appenines were abandoned. The women refused to stay and the few young farmers who were left had to send to the deep south for brides. A new profession – the rural marriage broker – appeared. Parliament had at last to register the demise of the share-cropping system which had been moribund for two decades. The political parties themselves had to revise their attitude to the southern question as it became clear that the peasants no longer wanted the land.

The first step in this great migration was to move away from the barren hilltops into the plains. Malaria had driven the people into the hills and its disappearance brought them down again. For a while the revival of agriculture in Campania, Metaponto and other places in the south brought prosperity as local food industries sprang up, but these new rural centres were soon swamped by the afflux of population from the hinterland, and when a crisis hit the small food industries in 1968 the result was tragic.

The experts noted that southern Italy was caught between two stools. She could compete neither with the cheap labour countries of the Mediterranean area nor with the streamlined agricultural industries of north-west Europe. In the late sixties Italy's food processing industries were evolving from the artisan level to that of the big international processing firms, with the result that technological unemployment came to aggravate the structural unemployment always present in the south. The big firms were ready, if expedient, to import their tomato pulp from the Ukraine rather than buy from the farms that had been financed by the land reform. The successful integration of efficient Italian industry in the markets of the affluent world was an additional source of hardship for the south. Hard money had been the fetish of Italian governments for twenty years – even when the Americans counselled devaluation to help employment – but in 1968 the experts at last admitted that the lira was too dear for the south. More than ever the southern economy had become dependent on outside capital and outside initiative and more than ever its needs were misunderstood by the north. In 1968 the chairman of the Confederation of Industries, a Genoese shipowner, opined that the south should now fend for itself. Everything that could be done for it had been tried.

The feeling of resignation and defeat was overtaking even the experts of the various planning bureaux, where the young men, no longer quite so young, were beginning to lose their enthusiasm. In twenty years £600m. had been spent on infrastructures for the south. Much of it had been wasted, for the money which filtered through the hands of the Cassa had all too often flowed into political channels. Public works were undertaken to bolster the prestige of local notables. Co-ordination and over-all planning were lacking, and the central authority – government, regional government or Cassa – was too weak to control the local pressure groups. At the worst the Mafia cut in and government aid was distorted for private gain; at the best it was spent for limited local ends which often contrasted with the over-all requirements of the region. When trouble broke out early in 1969 at Battipaglia, a small town in Campania hit by the rural economic crisis, Italy's leading agrarian economist, Manlio Rossi Doria, exclaimed sadly, 'We have no strategy for the south except emigration.'

Today new thinking is being applied to the industrial sector as well as to agriculture. Over $2,000m. have been invested in the south since 1950 and some four or five industrial development areas have proved viable. The most prosperous and self-propelling is the area around Naples and Salerno, where a number of engineering and other industries with a high ratio of manpower to capital investments have been set up. In Apulia the Bari–Brindisi–Taranto area is also beginning to grow, although the two basic industries of steel at Taranto and petrochemicals at Brindisi have not led to a proliferation of secondary activities as the experts appear to have hoped. But at Gela, where ENI set up its giant petrochemical establishment, the local environment – a depressed area of southern Sicily – proved unfavourable to further growth and the ENI mammoth stands alone.

A more flourishing development area has sprung up on the east coast of Sicily around the port of Augusta and the chemical industries of the Catania–Syracuse strip. Pescara on the Adriatic, and Latina near Rome are smaller centres where the incentives to local enterprise have borne fruit, probably because other favourable conditions were present. But after twenty years of incentives and investments in infrastructures – roads, ports, electricity and water supplies and the like – southern industry produces a bare fifteen per cent of the national industrial product and the gap between the growth rates of north and south continues to grow, while unemployment and underemployment are still chronic. The conviction is beginning to grow among the experts that what is good for northern industry is probably bad for the south. Pasquale Saraceno, the author of Italy's various development plans, now says the time has come to think less about competitivity and more about creating new jobs.

This change of thought would hardly have come about were it not for the fact that the south is becoming once again the scene of political unrest, on a wider scale and in a different context from the peasant movements of twenty years ago, but with similar manifestations of violence and hostility towards the state. People have woken up to the fact that large areas of the south are destined to stay outside the development areas, to remain for ever poor and stagnant with living standards below the European, sometimes below the Mediterranean norm. But the population is not resigned, as it once was, to ever-lasting hardship and humiliation. The Miracle brought television and the other mass media to even the poorest parts of the south. The impact of television in particular was revolutionary. No one in Italy today, however poor, is reconciled to living outside the 'consumer civilization' whose culture is propagated at every turn.

158

The most exasperated are the people who have seen prosperity moving towards them only to pass them by. This happened when natural gas was found in Ferrandina in Lucania, raising false hopes of an impossible industrial development after the building of one or two plants. It happened at Battipaglia in Campania when the tobacco and tomato canning factories closed down, throwing three thousand people out of work. It is happening almost daily in many parts of the south as the small industries fold up and the oranges and tomatoes have to be destroyed. New causes of anger and disappointment are added to the accumulated rancour of decades and the result is an explosion of wrath which takes the form of *jacquerie*, familiar to the south.

There have been seditious risings in one town after another since the winter of 1968-9. As a rule the population marches on the town hall, destroys the tax files and the city archives, sets fire to furniture, books, registers. Sometimes there is open conflict with the police. At Avola and Battipaglia shots were fired and people were killed. The chronicle of these risings reads exactly like the accounts of the great peasant rising of 1892, the Fasci Siciliani. Once again the enemy is not so much the landlord as the insensitive, slow-moving, pedantic, legalistic and hopelessly inefficient Italian state. The state that can never get help in time to the victims of earthquakes and floods, but is always ready to torment the citizen with its incessant demands for stamped documents to prove his right to work, to change his residence, to marry, to exist. The politicians make things worse by their absurd election promises and their solemnly repeated but ever eluded pledges to introduce reforms.

Perhaps the worst difficulty the Left-Centre governments have encountered – more insidious even than the economic sabotage of the conservatives – is the ingrained hostility of the bureaucracy with its stubborn, instinctive resistance to streamlining reforms. Ever since Parri's attempt to purge the civil service was frustrated in 1945 the bureaucrats have been a law unto themselves, a state within the state. Twelve ministers for the reform of the administration have sat in twelve successive cabinets but, in such a legal-minded community as Italy, any attempt to change the spirit of the civil service without first revising the laws it is called on to apply is like putting the cart before the horse. So far the only 'administrative' reforms that have got by are those imposed by the civil servants themselves to protect their careers.

Since 1963 the Left-Centre parties have stumbled into every sort of pitfall, from balance of payments troubles to financial and administrative sabotage and the non-co-operation of the unions. The socialists have often yielded to the temptation to adapt to the easy-going ways of a party in government and to feel that all that is required of them is to get as many of their own people as possible into the top places. They had promised and expected, by their mere presence, to be able to change the tone of government and they are probably more to blame than anyone for the failure to get the Left-Centre off the ground. As a formula for government it has proved very nearly as sterile and immobile as the Right-Centre coalition that preceded it.

All this would not matter so much if Italy, in addition to being an important industrial power with a big urban population, were also endowed with the welfare services and other attributes of modern democracies. But this is not so. Italy's health services, for instance, are expensive and cumbersome and are entirely in the hands of semi-independent insurance corporations, many of them immensely rich and all principally concerned with the business of providing high salaries and fat liquidation bonuses and pensions for their top-ranking administrators. In six years the corporations have stood out success-fully against the attempts of the socialist minister to co-ordinate and streamline the health service.

Similar frustrations and congestion attend the administration of justice. The law's delays in Italy – such is the clutter of business in the law courts – must be calculated in lustres, not in years. Twelve years is the accepted average for a civil law suit. For a penal offence a man may easily spend more time in prison awaiting trial than he is liable to receive as the maximum penalty if he is found guilty. If he happens to be innocent his case is sad indeed. The shortage of magistrates, the lack of facilities in the courts, the punctilious pedantry of the law are some of the causes of this blockage; of late

Map of the motorways

years the pressure of motoring offences has so bogged down the courts that the government has to resort to frequent amnesties to clear the backlog. Distrust of the law and its delays has become an additional cause of banditry in Sardinia (where magistrates are sent for punishment) and congestion of the city jails with young offenders awaiting trial has been the basic cause of prison riots in Milan, Turin and other big cities.

Congestion of the law courts, congestion of the hospitals, congestion of the prisons, of the schools and universities, of the streets: the fearful traffic jams that choke the big cities are a symbol of the frustrations the citizen encounters in all his dealings with the state. For twenty years and more Italy's unsolved problems have been allowed to pile up until they have begun to increase by geometrical progression under the pressure of urbanization and the new living standards created by the economic boom.

The main cause of this paralysis is political. It is the curse of coalition governments that they can never bring themselves to make decisions that are going to hurt. Parliament has become a filter whose purpose is to stop the reforms from getting through. Governments take only the easy decisions, those which are imposed upon them by a stronger will than their own, like the decision to build the great motorways, which was made less by government than by Fiat; for in this vacuum of political energy the real power centres are the big monopolistic industries, whether state-owned or private. In fact the industrial controversy has shifted from the polemic between the private and the public sectors, which was the pattern until Mattei's death in October 1962. Today there is a more subtle controversy between the really big industries – Fiat, Pirelli, ENI, IRI etc. – and the smaller industries still identified with the Confindustria. The difference of attitude is reflected in the newspapers. *La Stampa* and *Il Giorno*, which represent Fiat and ENI, usually take a broader view than the old-fashioned conservative papers which are still fighting a ghost battle for private enterprise. The giant industries are less prejudiced in their attitude towards the communists and this is what distinguishes them from the Confindustria. All they want is peace on the workshop floor and they are prepared to buy it at its political price which, at the turn of the decade, is support for the Left-Centre coalition with an eye open to the possibility of extending this to the communists.

For all these political and 'cultural' reasons the great motorways are the real symbol of contemporary Italy. From the outset the decision to build them was recognized as an alternative choice to building more schools and hospitals. The choice was imposed, almost without deliberate pressure, by the motor industry to which the Italian economy is at present tightly geared. It was accepted after a few murmurs by socialists and communists. Today the highways stand as superb pieces of engineering – very characteristic of the Italian genius for building roads, dams and aqueducts in every part of the globe. In time the motorways, particularly the great *Autostrada del Sole* built by IRI, may prove as important for linking together northern and southern Italy as the railways were. But the fact remains that they were very costly and they were built at the expense of other things, not just of schools and hospitals in the material sense but of bold, surgical, long overdue structural reforms. Education, justice, the health service, the tax system, the administration, the entire machinery of public life needs overhauling, and governments are afraid to tinker. The Left-Centre's grand reforms, like its development programme, have been whittled down and down and even so, at the first opposition in Parliament, they stall.

Of all the projected reforms none has aroused the emotional hostility of the conservatives more than the university reform project. This proposes to alter the present quasi-feudal system of university government in favour of a more democratic organization. The essence of it is that it will deprive some 3,000 chair-holding professors of the right of life and death inside the universities and in the professions of medicine law, architecture and engineering, where power and influence are concentrated in the hands of the big university *patrons*. These not only control all university appointments. They decide the curricula and dictate the law to 6,000 acting professors, 8,000 lecturers, 20,000 unpaid assistant lecturers and half a million students. The medical *patrons* also allocate to themselves the lion's share of the emoluments from the university clinics. The dissatisfaction of the medical lecturers and students has not unnaturally been a decisive factor in the students' movement. Under the present system academic authority and political influence are closely linked. One of the clauses of the reform bill which most riles the Establishment insists that university professors who are elected to Parliament must temporarily give up their chairs. There are over seventy such professors in Parliament and more than half are Christian Democrats. So far from giving up their chairs in the past, ministers have actually had chairs created for them in Rome University and occasionally take a day off from government to hold examinations. Thus the university is not only symbolically but physically linked to the 'system' the students denounce.

The students' movement began in Italy round about 1966. It begun with the tiny heretical marxist sects and its main centres were the universities of Turin, Venice, Pisa and Trento, in each of which the young people elaborated their own version of the doctrine of student power. Though it owes something to the example of Berkeley, Paris and Berlin, and to the ideas of Marcuse, the movement in its Italian context is spontaneous and autochthonous. It is not only a protest against the alienating character of the capitalist-consumer society but a specific protest against the authoritarian, paternalistic, hierarchical structure of Italian society and of Italian universities, which the students take to be mirrors and instruments of the 'system'.

In the winter of 1967-8 the movement became a rising and spread to the whole of Italy with student sit-ins, assemblies and countercourses (or anti-lessons) in which the students voiced their ideas, establishing two points of doctrine. They would have no centralized bureaucratic organization and they would not delegate their powers. The movement should have no officers or elected representatives but its assembly should be sovereign and permanent. This completely anarchist structure is a protest against Parliament and representative democracy, which the students reject as a sham. The lack of organization, however, has all but destroyed the movement, which is back again where it started, divided into sects and *groupuscules*. Its great moment of passion was in March 1968 when the police attacked the students outside the architecture faculty in Rome. The battle of Valle Giulia was their first and biggest conflict with the police but there have been many lesser scuffles since then and the police are in a state of permanent alert *vis-à-vis* the students, whom they most passionately hate. The quasi-pathological hostility of the police (who look on the students as a privileged class who delight in humiliating them) is one factor that still tends to keep the movement alive after the disappointments which followed the discomfiture of the students in Paris in May 1968.

In Italy today the movement is still looking for a strategy. It is uncertain whether to fold back upon itself and confine its attacks on the university or whether to concentrate on cultivating an alliance with the workers and seeking allies in the political parties on the extreme left (the PCI and the PSIUP). Relations between the movement and the Communist party are embarrassed. The students tend to look on the PCI as authoritarian and dogmatic, and as part of the Establishment no less than the Christian Democrats or the Confederation of Industries or the Church. For their part the communists feel they must show sympathy towards the students but are irritated by their refusal to take orders from the hierarchy. The movement is a heresy and as such the communists distrust it.

The student movement looks weak and divided in 1970 but its influence as a leaven upon Italian society should not be under-rated. The risings in southern Italy, the prison revolts, the demonstrations and strikes in the north all owe something to the new spirit of criticism that is coming out of the universities and the lycées. Many of the reforms the students demand are being granted even before the bill itself is passed. Teachers and professors are consenting to discuss the curricula and here and there the students have succeeded in imposing their own conception of the lycée or the university as a place where the generations can actually talk to each other. Will it last? Will it lead to anything? Will the Establishment (with or without the communists in government) get the upper hand? It is too soon to say. What matters at present is that youth, once so respectful of authority, so anxious to get on with the help of protection and recommendations in a society where influence is all, is

165

questioning the structure of that society. The conservatives are optimistic (in their ghoulish way). They believe the young people will settle down, that they will become integrated in the system once they have to fend for themselves. But should this prophecy prove wrong, should the young people keep up their contestation in spite of all the difficulties, the hostility of the police, the snares and pitfalls of partial reforms, should they insist on calling their elders to account for all the ills afflicting Italian society, then indeed we might see a spiritual breakthrough which could be the starting-point of a new era in Italian history.

12   The Italian scene

WHAT SORT OF PEOPLE are the Italians? A kindly critic of these pages tells me it is sometimes hard to see the people for the parties. But that is how Italians see themselves. They hate empiricism. For them philosophy is the highest discipline and ideological theory and doctrine, however imperfectly assimilated, are matters of the first importance, determining not only how a man votes but how he lives and the people he consorts with. No one in Italy can fail to belong to one or other of the country's political traditions and if he did, the Italian passion for classification would soon find a place for him. A man may be a catholic (integrationalist or liberal) or an anticlerical (liberal or radical) or a marxist (socialist or communist), or he may still be a fascist. Of course there are plenty of 'qualunquists', that is people who sneer at democracy and claim to mind their own business without embracing any political creed, but they are usually bracketed as potential fascists and despised as political outcasts. These divisions come naturally to Italians (the language itself can hardly refrain from adding an -ism to every concept) for they correspond to one of the very oldest Italian traditions, that of the factions whose partisan violence destroyed the medieval communes and prepared the way for the tyranny of the *signorie*, just as today they are destroying Italy's post-war parliamentary democracy. To most Italians the party or the faction is a more vivid reality than the vaguer idea of nation. It even takes precedence of a man's sentimental attachment to his native region. Often it is stronger than class.

American sociologists and historians sometimes refer to Italy as a 'segmented' society, by which they mean that loyalties are usually restricted to very small groups held together by strong personal ties. The family is the most important of these but it is followed closely by the patron-client relationship, which is very strong and is by no means restricted to the south although of course the Mafia is a striking example of it. The interclass structure of this peculiarly Italian system is illustrated by the way people used to live in the old patrician palaces. On the ground floor there were workshops for craftsmen and artisans; then came the *piano nobile* for the prince and his family. Above this was a less splendid suite of rooms for his dowager mother and finally the upper floors housed poor relations and hangers-on. This feudal but civilized pattern of living still lingers on in a few historic palaces though in Rome one may find American officials or foreign diplomats replacing the old retainers on the upper floors.

In many ways Sicily is a mirror for Italian society, the more revealing because it so often magnifies or distorts important features or even turns them upside down. Milazzo's junta in Palermo, for instance, was a parody of Left-Centre government in Rome. Sicily is like Italy only more so (as Goethe noticed nearly two centuries ago). Corruption is baser there, honour more jealous, and the typical Italian aspiration towards *signorilità*, which means the noble way of life, is grander in Sicily than elsewhere. That is why Lampedusa's novel *The Leopard* made such a tremendous impression on Italians – it told them things they knew but had never dared to say – and why Sicilian literature in general, from Verga and Pirandello to Brancati and Sciascia, is so important for understanding Italy. Lampedusa tells of the reluctance of Sicilians a century ago to believe they had anything to learn of the Piedmontese. In a different context this attitude persists, for one of Italy's greatest problems is how to weld her two cultures, the Western European and the Mediterranean.

The conflict between north and south goes deeper than mere friction between a progressive and a backward economy. Tens of thousands of southerners are living in spiritual isolation on the fringes of the great northern towns. Visconti's film *Rocco and his Brothers* depicts the drama of one such family and the panic despair of a young southern boy in his effort to 'conquer' the north. Naturally the most poignant conflicts concern the sex taboos and the

168

jealous code of honour of the south. This makes a man responsible not only for his wife's virtue but for that of all his womenkind. In fact the misdemeanour of a daughter or a sister comes even nearer home and can only be wiped out in blood. Italy's penal code, which was drawn up during fascism, tends to reflect the southern viewpoint and the penalties for avenging honour are very light. A man can get off with as little as two or three years for killing a faithless wife or her lover, and a woman can avenge her honour for approximately the same price. Italian films often poke fun at this state of affairs and Germi's brilliant satire, *Divorce Italian-style*, probably helped to start a movement to reform the penal code, but the draft bill to eliminate the *delitto d'onore* has still to get through Parliament and the minister of justice who proposed it received many threatening letters from the south. Until recently the virility cult and its obverse cult of female purity received encouragement from the Church but lately there has been a change of trend since Paul VI gave his blessing to a Sicilian girl who defied one of the island's more sinister sex laws (she refused to marry the young man who had kidnapped and raped her).

To change the mentality of the south and so break the power of the Mafia is Danilo Dolci's life work. For fifteen years this extraordinary man has been campaigning in the slums of Palermo and the little Mafia towns of western Sicily. For a long time he seemed to be making no headway at all and though his name was widely known abroad few people inside Italy had heard of him. Again and again, by hunger strikes and other forms of peaceful demonstration, he drew the attention of the outside world to the abuses of the Mafia and the connivance of the Sicilian (and the Italian) Establishment. Today something in the nature of a psychological breakthrough is building up in the south though it may not be as peaceful as Dolci would like. The task he has set himself is herculean, nothing less than to persuade Italians that things can change simply because enough people – ordinary people without special power and influence – want them to be different; but to do this he has to destroy the ingrained conviction of Italians, northerners and southerners alike, that the only way to get things done is by pulling strings. For this very reason public opinion in Italy counts for little or nothing. Democracy has not changed this fact. In twenty years innumerable scandals have come to light but seldom have the people responsible for them been brought to book and it is more often the accusers, not the accused, who land in jail. In six years the Mafia Commission itself has been unable to pin down a single accusation, whereas Dolci and his fellow workers have often been condemned for slander. Pessimism engenders defeatism, and Italian writers in the past have sometimes mistaken this for patience and resignation and extolled these as Italian virtues. Whether they are virtues or not these attributes are not as typical of southern Italy as they used to be.

Industrial paternalism is the northern version of the Italian 'system', with the firm standing in for the family or the personal clientèle as the basic unit or segment. None of the older industrial countries have developed welfare institutions on such exclusively paternalistic lines. The spirit behind this phenomenon is very similar to that which inspired the Jesuits of old to build their great baroque churches and to lay on music and entertainment as well as providing schools and hospitals so as to surround the faithful with an atmosphere of protection and comfort from which, at any moment, the disobedient could be ejected into hell. In a somewhat similar way the big Italian firms hold out the threat of banishment from the comforts and security they supply. Every sort of amenity is laid on, from crèches and maternity wards to technical schools and grade A football teams. All the Italian love of magnificence and feeling for style are poured into the buildings. The Olivetti buildings in particular, both at Pozzuoli and at Ivera, are models of sophisticated industrial architecture.

Some of these firms, like Olivetti, Marzotto, Fiat and ENI, have created their own communities in which every physical and spiritual need is taken care of except a man's right to call his soul his own. Small towns like Ivrea or Valdagno are modern versions of the *signoria* with the firm taking the place of the duke even to the point of patronizing the arts. Their prizes for painting, sculpture, poetry and so forth carry national and international prestige. Even a large town like Turin, with a population of close on a million, is in fact the feudal domain of Fiat and reflects the enlightened despotism of the firm, while ENI has built a city in its own image – Metanopoli – on the outskirts of Milan. From a sense of duty quite as much as from expediency all these big firms have turned (or are turning) their attention to the south, but curiously enough the southerners are proving less amenable than northern Italians to the blandishments of industrial paternalism. Perhaps for the very reason that the older pattern of society, with its complicated network of loyalties, is stronger there, people find it hard to transfer their allegiance to a firm.

One of the features that makes Italy so attractive to foreigners (particularly from the north) is the absence of chauvinism or indeed of any sort of self-righteousness. Italians do not believe that God is necessarily on their side. At the best they hope for a good word from the Virgin. The nationalism that gave birth to fascism was never a manifestation of self-confidence but the reverse. Like the English, the Italians are given to self-mockery but the tone of this is a great deal more bitter. To do things *all'italiana* means to rush ahead without serious preparation or forethought, perhaps to bluff. A young man who had been taken prisoner in World War II told me afterwards: 'Of course we knew that Mussolini's wooden cannons were a bluff. But we hoped the others were bluffing too.'

To understand the Italians, and discover a common denominator between north and south, one should look at the tradition of the Commedia dell'Arte and its modern version, the Italian comic film. There are a number of actors – outstanding among them is Alberto Sordi, but one also thinks of Gassman and of the Neapolitan Edoardo de Flippo, the last and perhaps the greatest of Italy's Pulcinellas, or of Marcello Mastroianni, the prototype of the Italian *bell'Antonio*, of Manfredi and Tognazzi – each of whom, in his own way, has created a 'mask' through which he expresses what is pathetic, exasperating, touching or endearing in the foibles of the Italian male; his vanity, his desire to cut a fine figure, to please and to impress, his willingness to flatter, his essential kindness, his attachment to domestic joys and, most important of all, his deep sense of compassion for human frailty. Perhaps this, more than any other trait, is the key to Italian behaviour; the law's delays in Italy are very long but, when it comes, Italian justice is more merciful than ours. Two films come to mind which illustrate the Italian spirit and the way sophisticated Italians look at their own plight. One is Mario Monicelli's film *The Great War*, which stars both Gassman and Sordi and tells the story of two privates in World War I who end up as heroes although all they wanted was to save their skins. Somehow these two tragi-comic figures stand in for all the millions of Italians who have been betrayed and pushed around by a rhetorical, incompetent establishment ever since Italy became united. The other film is Fellini's *Vitelloni* (The Young Bloods), an exquisite description of the boredom and despair that assails the young men in a dead-end provincial town.

Life is sweet under the Italian sun but it can also be very bitter and the macaroni image is misleading. Even this humble dish is a luxury for many Italians whose staple diet is bread and chicory. In any case how can one generalize about a people which, in our own time, has produced types as different as Mussolini and Pope John? Ever since they began to emerge as a nation the Italians presented contrasting facets. Which is more typical of the national genius, Dante on his austere quest for truth and perfection or Boccaccio bubbling over with laughter at the human scene? Saint Francis preaching love and humility or Savonarola threatening fire and brimstone, Macchiavelli urging the Italians to make a desperate stand or Guicciardini advising them to stay at home and keep out of trouble? Which is the real Italy, the country that rose in the Risorgimento and the Resistance or the nation of trimmers that accepted fascism and now lives under Christian Democracy? They both exist, they are both real, and as things go, they are probably both eternal.

Abbreviations

AGIP   State petroleum prospecting and operating agency (*Agenzia Generale Italiana di Petrolio*)

CGIL   General confederation of Italian workers (*Confederazione Generale Italiana del Lavoro*)

CISL   Catholic confederation of trade unions (*Confederazione Italiana dei Sindicati Lavoratori*)

CLNAI   North Italian liberation committee (*Comitato di Liberazione Nazionale Alt' Italia*)

ENI   National hydrocarbon corporation (*Ente Nazionale Idrocarburi*)

FUCI   Catholic federation of university students (*Federazione degli Universitari Cattolici Italiani*)

IMI   Italian investment institute (*Istituto Mobiliare Italiano*)

IRI   Institute for industrial reconstruction (*Istituto della Ricostruzione Industriale*)

MSI   Neo-fascist party (*Movimento Sociale Italiano*)

OVRA   Fascist secret police (*Opera Vigilanza e Repressioni Antifascisti*)

PCI   Italian communist party (*Partito Communista Italiano*)

PNF   Fascist party (*Partito Nazionale Fascista*)

PSDI   Social Democratic party *Partito Socialista Democratico Italiano*

PSI   Socialist party (*Partito Socialista Italiana*)

PSIUP   Socialist Unity party (*Partito Socialista Italiano di Unità Proletaria*)

SIFAR   Military counter-espionage service (*Servizio Informazione delle Forze Armate*)

UIL   Social-democratic labour federation (*Unione Italiana del Lavoro*)

173

Notes on the Text

1 *The City of the Sun* was written while Campanella was in prison. Inspired by Plato, it describes an ideal state in which men share their goods and their wives and are ruled by philosopher-priests who teach them wisdom and love.

1 The population in Italy, after the incorporation of Venetia and Latium, was 27 million in 1870.

2 This injunction, contained in a decree of 1874, was known as the *non expedit*. It was never formally revoked but in 1905 an encyclical of Pius X allowed catholics to take part in public life when special circumstances recognized by the bishops justified it.

3 Alarmed by the insurrection of February 1848, King Charles Albert of Sardinia granted his subjects a constitution. The 'Statute' promulgated by him on 4 March claimed to be the 'fundamental, perpetual and irrevocable' law of the monarchy. The form of parliamentary government it sanctioned was regarded by the King as a concession made from the fullness of his sovereignty. Later, Cavour and the liberals liked to think that Italy was a constitutional monarchy in which sovereignty was vested in Parliament, that is in the King and the Chambers. In March 1861 the Statute was extended to the new kingdom of Italy, which the monarchy always regarded as the continuation and extension of the old kingdom of Sardinia and Piedmont. No machinery had been devised to safeguard the constitution, so that later on the fascist régime was able to abrogate or modify the rules laid down by the Statue without resort to special legislation. Hence the desire, in 1946–47, for a more rigid constitution.

4 Attached to the Encyclical *Quanta Cura,* the Syllabus denounced 80 'principal errors of our time'. In particular it rejected the idea that the

Roman pontiff should become reconciled to and agree with 'progress, liberalism and modern civilization'. It denied the doctrine of the sovereignty of the people, and refused to accept the separation of Church and state or agree to the equal status of all religions before the law. In Italy the Syllabus undermined the position of the liberal catholics and created a breach between the Church and the intellectuals.

5 The Law of Guarantees proposed to define the prerogatives of the Supreme Pontiff and the relations between the Church and the Italian state. The Pope's position was to be sacred and his person inviolable and he was to be given the style and prerogatives of a sovereign with free access for his couriers and diplomatic immunity for foreign representatives attached to his court. An annuity of 3 million lire was promised him and the state gave up its old jurisdictional rights over the Church. Bishops no longer had to swear fealty to the king. The Law of Guarantees, whose validity the Pope refused to accept, was an internal law of the Italian state, not a treaty.

6 Stefano Jacini noted this 'monstrous' marriage of British liberalism with authoritarian French centralization.

7 Vincenzo Gioberti (1801–52) was a catholic philosopher whose thinking was influential in the 1840's in obtaining the support of liberal catholics for the national idea. He identified religion with civilization and believed that Italy should be united as a federation of states under the spiritual and political leadership of the Pope. The past greatness of Italy, he thought, had been the work of the Church and the Risorgimento could only succeed if it became grafted onto catholic tradition. In his *Moral and Civil Primacy of the Italians* (1843) he solicited the advent of an enlightened pontiff who would bring catholicism into harmony with modern ideas of civil progress.

8 He was given command of an improvised Armée des Vosges which fought at Dijon in the only victorious action on the French side of the entire Franco–Prussian war.

9 Various pieces of the dissolving Turkish empire were dangled before Italy at the Congress but Count Corti, the Italian representative, refused to become involved in the scramble and boasted that he had come through it with clean hands. See C. Seton-Watson, *Italy from Liberalism to Fascism*, pp. 104–6.

10 Fiat, Italy's big motor industry, was born in 1895.

11 Emilio Visconti-Venosta (1829–1914) was foreign minister 1876–86. His remark is quoted by F. Chabod in *La Politica Estera Italiana 1871–96*.

12   Crispi was prime minister from August 1887 to February 1891 and again December 1893 to March 1896.

13   Emigration became a mass phenomenon after 1870, averaging 123,000 emigrants a year, only 6.6% of whom came from the south. Overseas emigration increased rapidly in the eighties and nineties. The total emigration average for 1887–1900 was 269,000 a year. France was the principal receiving country in Europe. In America by 1900 the U.S. were taking more Italian emigrants than Argentina and Brazil. Between 1900 and 1913 emigration averaged 626,000 a year (46% from the south). In the peak year 1913 873,000 Italians left the country. Blocked by the U.S. after 1920, Italian emigration turned to France and Switzerland. Between 1919 and 1927 over a million Italians emigrated to France. The Fascist régime discouraged emigration (very partially replaced by colonization of the African territories). The average from 1933 to 1937 was a bare 52,000 a year. After World War II there was a revival of emigration overseas to Canada and Australia but West Germany and Switzerland soon became the principal markets for Italian labour. In the five-year period 1960–65 Italy sent 655,000 workers to Switzerland and 490,000 to West Germany as against 75,000 to Canada and 73,000 to Australia. In 1965 it was reckoned that Italy had over three million workers abroad (with their families equal to at least six million souls). These are the highest emigration figures in the world. The average benefit to the Italian balance of payments is over £300 million a year.

3   LIBERAL DECLINE

1   The Italian trade-union movement developed out of the leagues and fraternities of the 19th century. The General Confederation of Labour (CGIL) was set up in 1906 but although the Socialists had considerable influence on the movement they never actually controlled the unions, which were jealous of their autonomy. Revolutionary syndicalism inspired by Sorel developed inside the Confederation and in 1912 the revolutionary syndicalists, who thought the main purpose of trade-union action was to prepare the workers for revolution, set up their own federations which contributed, after World War I, to the development of fascist corporativism. A catholic trade-union movement developed after 1898, giving birth in 1918 to a federation of catholic unions. All these federations were dissolved after the advent in 1925 of the Confederation of Fascist Corporations.

2   The word *Fascio*, which means a sheaf, was commonly used before

1920 to denote a league or association. After 1893 it acquired a flavour of social revolution.

3 Mussolini had no reason to fear a blockade in 1922 but he underestimated the effect of sanctions on the Italian economy in 1935.

4 The modernist movement which developed at the beginning of the century inside the Roman Catholic Church sought to adapt the catholic religion to the requirements of modern culture and progress on the assumption that the Christian message is subject to continual evolution in order to remain in harmony with a changing cultural environment. In Italy the movement had political connotations. It was condemned as a heresy by Pius X in 1907 and an anti-modernist oath was exacted from suspect priests and catholic intellectuals.

5 The influence of local notables on elections, particularly in the south, has survived into the present era of universal (including women's) suffrage. It is a consequence of the segmentation of Italian society into groups or clienteles each of which gravitates upon some outstanding local personality whose influence stems from the power to dispose of patronage.

6 Brigandage and unrest in the southern provinces after the unification drew the attention of several outstanding economists and reformers to the fact that political union with northern Italy was actually damaging the south. These so-called *meridionalisti* sought to bring the southern question to the notice of government and of public opinion on the assumption that good will and a few tariff and fiscal reforms could correct the distortions and injustice affecting the south. Pasquale Villari (1826–1917) was the first to point out the deficiencies and incomprehension of the central government in a series of letters from the south. In the seventies Luigi Franchetti and Sidney Sonnino conducted two masterly inquiries into conditions in the Neapolitan provinces and in Sicily. Giustino Fortunato (1848–1932) was perhaps the greatest of the *meridionalisti*, the first to point out the existence of two Italies, climatically and physically different, and to present the southern question as the central problem of Italian life. Salvemini was the first to approach it in political terms. He deplored the corruption encouraged by Giolitti and advocated a wide suffrage which would allow illiterate peasants to have representatives in parliament, an idea not welcomed by the Socialist party at that time. Salvemini wanted the southern peasants to form an alliance with the industrial workers of the north. This idea was taken up by the communist leader Antonio Gramsci, who also ranks among the *meridionalisti* although his position is singular. He saw the alliance between

peasants and workers in terms of revolutionary action but vainly hoped for co-operation from the southern intellectuals. Guido Dorso (1892–1947) was the last of the genuine *meridionalisti*. Like Salvemini, he imagined that the revolution of the south could be achieved in the political framework of democracy. The *meridionalisti* were individual reformists – even Gramsci found little support from his party. Thanks to their dedication and to their vigorous intellectual stature – their place in Italian letters is as outstanding as in social history – the southern question was universally accepted as one, if not *the* central, problem of the Italian Republic after World War II, and has become the object of collective study and special institutions, first and foremost the Cassa per il Mezzogiorno set up in 1950.

7 Cesare Balbo (1789–1853) was a historian and political writer of the early Risorgimento. In *Speranze d'Italia* (1844) he developed the theory that Piedmont should become the fulcrum of the new Italy and that the Habsburg empire should expand eastwards into the Balkans in order to leave room for Italy to move into Lombardy and Venetia.

4   WAR AND PEACE

1 Arturo Labriola (1873–1959) was a leader of the revolutionary syndicalist movement and, like Mussolini, an admirer of Sorel. He believed in the revolutionary function of the workers' unions and the need for them to keep their autonomy within the socialist fold. In 1911 he thought the colonial war would be an opportunity to prepare the workers for revolutionary action. Revolutionary syndicalism contributed not a little to fascist ideology but Labriola himself changed his views and in 1926 left Italy (and the chair of economics at Messina University) as an anti-fascist.

2 Filippo Tommaso Marinetti (1876–1944) was the author of the 'manifesto' of 1909, published in the Paris *Figaro*, which marked the birth of the futurist movement. In Italy, the movement counts some outstandng painters, such as Boccioni, Severini and Carrà, but its political influence was deleterious and its literary manifestations – it claimed to abolish syntax – were often absurd. Futurism developed during the early years of motoring and aviation and exalted aggressiveness and speed. At the political level it produced the cult of action for action's sake and led to the glorification of war. It became a sort of cultural cradle for nationalism and later for fascism. Marinetti stood by Mussolini from the start and was rewarded with a place in the Academy.

178

3 Cesare Battisti (1875–1916) was a hero of Italian irredentism. Born in Trento under Habsburg rule, he founded a socialist paper which demanded administrative autonomy for the Trentino and an Italian university in Trento. In 1911 he became a deputy in the Austrian parliament but left Austria for Milan on the outbreak of war in order to make propaganda for Italian intervention. He enrolled in an alpine regiment in 1915 and a year later was taken prisoner by the Austrians, court-martialled as a traitor, and hanged.

5 INTO FASCISM

1 The Italian Communist party was born of a split which occurred during the Socialist party congress in Leghorn in January 1921. The communist motion in favour of strict obedience to Moscow polled 58,783 votes out of a total of 171,106. Serrati and the maximalists obtained the majority with 98,028. Turati and the reformists were left with 14,695 votes. The Communists walked out of the Goldoni theatre, where the congress was sitting, to set up a party of their own.

6 THE LEGACY OF FASCISM

1 In addition to Gramsci's *Ordine Nuovo* and Gobetti's *Rivoluzione Liberale,* both of which continued to appear in 1925, a new radical anti-fascist paper, *Non Mollare* (Don't Yield), was set up in Florence by Salvemini, C. Rosselli and Ernesto Rossi in 1925. It ceased publication when the editors were arrested. October 1925 also saw the end of G. Amendola's anti-fascist newspaper *Il Mondo,* edited by Alberto Cianca.
2 Carmine Senise (1883–1958) had retired as chief of police when he organized Mussolini's arrest. He returned to the post a few weeks later under Badoglio but was arrested and interned by the Germans.
3 In 1915 Mussolini had contracted civil marriage with Rachele Guidi who bore him five children.
4 The 'long journey' from fascism to communism is described by Ruggero Zangrande, *Il lungo viaggio attraverso il fascismo,* Milan, 1962.

7 BIRTH OF THE REPUBLIC

1 See Ruggero Zangrandi, *1943: 23 luglio – 8 settembre,* Milan, 1964. The behaviour of all the leading characters in this drama is still the subject of controversy and litigation. Zangrandi suggests that General Roatta (Chief of Staff of the Army in 1943) was later blackmailed (with the threat of handing him over to the Yugoslavs as a war criminal) into accepting the role of scapegoat for the failure to defend Rome.

8   CHRISTIAN DEMOCRACY

1   See R. A. Webster, *The Cross and the Fasces. Christian Democracy and Fascism in Italy* (Stanford University Press, 1960), Ch. 12. The University, founded by Father Agostino Gemelli in 1921, obtained government recognition from Mussolini in 1924. It controlled a publishing house, a lycée and a scientific review and its influence with the north Italian bourgeoisie was immense. Its politics sought to identify fascist corporativism with catholic social doctrine; it favoured fascist imperialism by appealing to the theories of living space and geopolitics, and it tried to justify the anti-Jewish laws as a defence of catholic tradition. Fanfani, who was professor of economics at the university, wrote a textbook on the significance of corporativism and defended fascist imperialism and the 'purity of the race' in articles in *Rivista internazionale di scienza sociale*.

2   See the essay by P. A. Allum on the political ecology of Naples in *Partiti politici e strutture sociali in Italia* (Edizioni di Communità, Milan, 1968). Mr Allum points out that when the Scelba government required the help of the eight monarchist deputies in the Chamber, an understanding was reached with the monarchist mayor of Naples, Achille Lauro, whereby special funds were made available to the local monarchist party for propaganda, thanks to which the party doubled its strength in the municipal elections of 1958.

3   Following a law passed in November 1969, the first ordinary regional elections are scheduled to take place simultaneously with the administrative elections in the spring of 1970.

4   Dennis Healey alone protested in 1947 that Saragat had fatally weakened Italian socialism.

9   ITALY FACES WEST

1   In May 1944 representatives of the French and Italian Resistance signed a declaration that no motive of resentment for the past subsisted between the two peoples, both of whom had been victims of oppression and corruption. The declaration ended with a pledge of complete solidarity and fraternity in the struggle to restore democratic freedom and social justice in a 'free European community'.

10   RIGHT CENTRE, LEFT CENTRE

1   Ernesto Rossi's pungent attacks on the malpractices of the Christian Democrat 'sub-government', the Confederation of Industries, the hierarchy etc. appeared first in the weekly paper *Il Mondo* and later in his own *L'Astrolabio* as well as in numerous books, of which *I Padroni del Vapore*

is the best-known. His letters from the *confino*, published posthumously in 1968, rank as a postscript to the literature of the Risorgimento.
2   On IRI and ENI see M. V. Posner and S. J. Woolf, *Italian Public Enterprise*, London, 1967.
3   The prolonged and staggered strikes of autumn 1969 in the engineering and chemical industries may produce a change of attitude. Big industry has lost confidence in the capacity of the Left-Centre leaders – socialist or Christian democrat – to keep peace in the factories through their control of the unions, and the same doubt applies to the communists and the CGIL. At present industry would like to see the unions more powerful and less scared of the workers.

II   THE MIRACLE FADES

1   The unification was short-lived. In April 1969 the social democrats again hived off from the united party on the pretext that the new majority in the PSI was preparing to bring the communists into the government. The accusation was unfounded and the real reason for the split is to be sought in personal and faction rivalries. The new social-democratic party, which is much weaker than the old – it has not carried with it the leaders of the social-democratic trade-union federation – calls itself Partito Socialista Unitaria, or PSU.

Acknowledgments

Associated Press, 33; Civica Raccolta delle Stampe, Milan, 3; George Eastman House, Rochester, N.Y., 6; ENI, Rome, 16; ENIT, London, 19, 26, 28; EPT, Potenza, 30; *Espresso*, 8, 14, 29; Fiat, 27; Joseph H. Hirshhorn Collection, New York, 21; Imperial War Museum, 13; Mansell Collection, 4; *Messaggero*, 7, 9; Mondadori, 2, 5, 11; Museo del Risorgimento, Rome, 1; National Film Archive, 18; Pier Luigi Nervi, 22; Olivetti, 31; Pirelli, 23; Presidenza del Consiglio, Rome, 10, 12, 15, 17, 24, 25, 32; UPI, 34.

181

Select Bibliography

Kogan, Norman, *A Political History of Postwar Italy*, London and New York, 1966. *The Politics of Italian Foreign Policy*, New York, 1963. *Italy and the Allies*, Cambridge, Mass., 1956. All three are important: Kogan has a flair for explaining the motives and mechanism of Italian politics.

Mammarella, Giuseppe, *Italy after Fascism. A Political History*, Montreal, 1964. Good on the relationship between Italy and the Americans.

Webster, Richard, *Christian Democracy in Italy, 1860–1960*, London, 1961.

Mack Smith, Denis, *Italy. A Modern History*, Michigan, 1959.

Seton Watson, Christopher, *Italy from Liberalism to Fascism, 1870–1925*, London, 1967.

Deakin, F. W., *The Last Days of Mussolini*, Harmondsworth, 1966.

Sprigge, Cecil, *The Development of Modern Italy*, London, 1943.

Albrecht-Carrié, R., *Italy from Napoleon to Mussolini*, New York, 1950. An excellent analysis of the historical chain of cause and effect that led to Fascist Italy.

Chabod, Frederico, *L'Italie Contemporaine*, Paris, 1950. Lectures delivered at the Sorbonne in 1950; recommended.

Santarelli, Enzo, *Storia del movimento e del regime fascista*, Rome, 1967.

Spriano, Paolo, *Storia del partito communista italiano*, 2 vols., Turin, 1967, 1969.

De Felice, Renzo, *Mussolini il revoluzionario*, Turin, 1966. *Mussolini il fascista*, Turin, 1968.

Jemolo, A. C., *Chiesa e stato in Italia negli cento anni*, revised ed., Turin, 1965.

Battaglia, R., *Storia della Resistenza italiana*, Turin, 1953.

Who's Who

CATTANEO, Carlo (1801–1869), economist, historian and political thinker. The influence of his federalist and republican ideas upon succeeding generations of Italians was second only to that of Mazzini. Before 1848 he advocated setting up Lombardy and Venetia as an independent unit in a federation of peoples subject to Austria. Later he thought of the whole of Italy in terms of an independent federation and in September 1848 he envisaged including this in a wider United States of Europe. He took active part in some outstanding events of the Risorgimento. In 1848 he was head of the council of war during the five days' insurrection in Milan and in September 1860 he was political adviser to Garibaldi in Naples, where he vainly urged federation of the south instead of annexation. The positivist school of Italian historiography starts with Cattaneo. His influence upon Salvemini was enormous and through Salvemini's disciples it reached the radical anti-fascists and penetrated into the Italian Resistance.

CAVOUR, Camillo Benso, Conte di (1810–1861) is rightly considered, together with Mazzini and Garibaldi, as one of the chief makers of united Italy, although what he really worked for, as prime minister to the King of Sardinia, was the creation of a large north Italian kingdom which should gravitate upon Piedmont. In this plan Lombardy and Venetia were to be taken from Austria with the help of French arms. The most brilliant diplomat in Europe since Talleyrand, Cavour sought to induce Napoleon III to attack Austria, but Napoleon disappointed him at Villafranca by leaving Venetia in Austrian hands. The popular risings in central Italy in 1860 obliged Cavour to alter his sights and to include the duchies of Tuscany, Modena and Parma in his greater Piedmont. He still hoped the Bourbon kingdom in the south could be preserved and the

183

assistance he gave Garibaldi for the expedition to Sicily was probably given in the hope that the hero and his enterprise would come to grief. Garibaldi's success in Sicily and Naples and the danger of a republican take-over in the south forced Cavour to make a virtue of necessity and to send King Victor Emmanuel post haste to seize Umbria and the Marches before Garibaldi took them or attacked the Pope. In spite of his liberal principles (based on admiration of the British parliamentary system), Cavour did not wait for the plebiscites to send his agents to take over the administration of the new territories but he died before his plans for the government of united Italy could be more than outlined. For a man of such rare political talent he was extraordinarily ingenuous in supposing that the papacy could accept his proposition of a free Church in a free State.

GARIBALDI, Giuseppe (1807–1882) was the most attractive and out-standing figure of the Italian Risorgimento and probably the most decisive. His legendary expedition to Sicily in 1860 with a thousand volunteers was the turning-point in the story of the unification. Without it the Bourbon territories in the south might never have been joined to the northern kingdom. Garibaldi was a republican at heart but he put the cause of national unity above everything. In his youth he joined Mazzini's 'Young Italy' and later spent fourteen adventurous years as a political exile in South America, where he established his reputation as a brilliant commander of guerrillas. News of the Palermo rising of 1848 brought him back to Italy with his volunteers in time to take part in the defence of the Roman Republic. The rout of the republican army and the tragic flight to San Marino (during which he lost his wife Anita) may have convinced him that national unity could never be achieved by the re-publican forces alone, and in 1856 he made his peace with the monarchy, though he was too loyal himself to understand how much King Victor Emmanuel II and Cavour distrusted him. In the war of 1859 he command-ed a volunteer corps which liberated Brescia, but the peace of Villafranca (which left Venice to Austria) disgusted him and he withdrew to his island home on Caprera. The Sicilian rising of 1860 was the signal for his return. The famous expedition of the Thousand was organized and set sail from Genoa with the tacit consent of the Piedmontese government, which neither expected nor greatly desired it to succeed, for most of the legionaries were ardent republicans. Garibaldi's extraordinary success, the ease with which he took Palermo and pushed on to Naples, alarmed

Cavour and obliged King Victor Emmanuel to forestall him by liberating Abruzzo and the Marches. The two heroes met at Teano and later entered Naples together but Garibaldi's role in Italian history henceforth was to be marginal.

MAZZINI, Giuseppe (1805–1872) is one of the most outstanding figures of the Italian Risorgimento, as essential as Garibaldi and Cavour. While a political exile in France, in 1831 he drew up the programme of 'Young Italy', an association that was to free Italy from foreign and domestic tyranny and make it a single independent republic. He had a mystical conception of the nation as the spirit or conscience of the people but he wanted the nations to be brothers and in 1834 he founded 'Young Europe'. In exile, mainly in London, he kept up a vast and incessant correspondence to keep the flame of revolution alive and promoted a number of abortive plots whose lack of success at first left his influence and prestige unimpaired. He claimed that even an insurrection that fails is a victory of the spirit of freedom. In March 1849 he was chosen a triumvir of the Roman Republic and showed unexpected capacity in organizing the resistance to the siege. Back in exile in the fifties he resumed his plotting but with the failure of Pisacane's expedition in 1857 his influence began to wane. The Risorgimento was turning royalist but Mazzini, unlike Garibaldi, would not conform. His last years were bitter for he was still under sentence of death in Italy and was arrested in 1870.

LIBERAL ITALY 1871–1922

CRISPI, Francesco (1819–1901), the second of Italy's 'parliamentary dictators', began his career as a Sicilian patriot and republican in contact with Mazzini and Garibaldi. Political organizer of Garibaldi's expedition in 1860. In parliament he sat with the Left, became reconciled to the monarchy, and succeeded Depretis as prime minister in 1887. With disastrous consequences he pushed to their extremes the policies of industrial protectionism and colonial expansion adopted by the Left. During his second ministry (1893–96) the skirmishes in Abyssinia developed into a full-scale war, which ended abruptly with the defeat of the Italians at Adowa, an event that brought about Crispi's fall. At home he showed great severity in suppressing the social risings which were in part a consequence of the distress caused by the effects of his tariffs. For his imperialistic ambitions and his authoritarianism Crispi is sometimes considered a forerunner of Mussolini, but the comparison is not wholly fair.

185

DEPRETIS, Agostino (1813–1887), the first of the so-called 'parliamentary dictators', became prime minister when the Left took over from the Right in 1876. He was the first to develop the 'trasformismo' system, trimming or expanding his majority to right or left as occasion demanded. In 1882 he concluded the Triple Alliance with Germany and Austria and began a policy of colonial expansion. At home his government broadened the franchise and abolished the unpopular grist tax. He remained in office with brief intervals until his death but was always in control of the majority thanks, in part, to the practice of corrupting the deputies from the south.

GIOLITTI, Giovanni (1841–1928), the third and most prestigious of the 'parliamentary dictators', dominated the political scene from 1901 to 1914. His first ministry (1892–3) was cut short by a bank scandal but in 1901 he became minister of the interior and was prime minister of three governments between 1903 and 1914. Throughout those years he controlled a majority in parliament, partly by bribing the deputies from the south. More enlightened than his contemporary conservatives, he saw the need to make concessions to the workers in industry and refrained from using violence to stop the strikes. His 'system' consisted in courting the reformist socialists – in 1903 he offered a ministry to Turati – while leaving the peasants to the mercy of the landowners whose interests he favoured by his tariffs on wheat. In foreign policy he was loyal to the Triple Alliance but cultivated better relations with France. He disliked colonial adventures and distrusted the nationalists but in 1911 he led the country into war in Libya in order to appease the Right. The colonial war put an end to Giolitti's system which could only work so long as the reformists controlled the Socialist Party. Giolitti had favoured a widening of the suffrage and tried to replace the socialists by an agreement with the catholics. In 1914 he was out of office and opposed Italian intervention in the war. His last government (1920–21) put an end to the quarrel with Yugoslavia but, under-estimating the danger from the Fascists, in 1921 he called the 'infernal election' which brought them into parliament.

LABRIOLA, Antonio (1843–1904). The first Italian scholar to undertake a systematic study of Marx, to which he contributed his own personal elaboration of the theory of historical materialism. His ideas greatly influenced the thinking of Benedetto Croce, like him a product of the Neopolitan school of Hegelian philosophy founded by De Sanctis and

186

Bertrando Spaventa. Even more important politically was Labriola's influence on the ideas of Antonio Gramsci (q.v.).

SELLA, Quintino (1827–1884) was finance minister in various post-unification governments between 1862 and 1873 when the wars of the Risorgimento had left the new kingdom so badly in debt that its financial, and hence political, independence was in danger. Sella built up the reserves and organized the nation's finances establishing the principle that a balanced budget must take precedence of every other consideration, a tradition that was revived by Luigi Einaudi during the period of reconstruction after World War II.

FASCIST AND ANTI-FASCIST ITALY 1922–43

CROCE, Benedetto (1866–1952), philosopher and liberal historian, exercised enormous influence, both cultural and political, on at least two generations of Italian intellectuals. Though inclined at first to tolerate the fascists, he soon changed his mind and drafted the manifesto of anti-fascist intellectuals in 1925. He was not greatly molested by the régime, partly on account of his international reputation as the most illustrious representative of the idealist school of philosophy but also because the type of intellectual resistance he preached was not considered dangerous. In 1944 he sat in the Badoglio and Bonomi governments and tried to persuade the King to abdicate in order to save the monarchy.

D'ANNUNZIO, Gabriele (1863–1938), poet and political adventurer, exercised an extraordinary influence both on the aesthetic taste of his generation and on the course of Italian history. After dominating the literary scene for twenty years with the outpourings of his turgid genius, he tried to put his fantasies into action and began by whipping up irredentist feelings towards Dalmatia as part of the lost Venetian empire. His Adriatic orientation supplied the nationalist movement with one of its most powerful myths; later he was to provide the fascists with the model for their tactics and their ideology as well as their black folklore, which derived from his organization of the Arditi, the volunteer corps of shock troops from whom his followers were largely drawn. In 1915 his campaign in favour of intervention was a factor in persuading the nation to enter the war, but after Versailles he complained of the 'mutilated victory' which deprived Italy of the promised spoils in Dalmatia. In September 1919 he marched on Fiume with a handful of volunteers, seized the town and set up a dictatorship. His exploit caused embarrassment to the government, but he was dislodged without bloodshed in December 1920 thanks to the connivance of Mussolini.

GENTILE, Giovanni (1875–1944) was an idealist philosopher whose national influence was inferior only to that of Croce, with whom he collaborated for twenty years. Unlike Croce, Gentile saw fascism as the continuation rather than the antithesis of the Risorgimento and hoped it would act as a corrective to the excessive individualism he believed the Italians had inherited from the Renaissance. As minister of education (1922–24) in Mussolini's first government he introduced a reform of school curricula which left a mark on two generations of Italians. He took no further part in politics during the régime but promoted cultural initiatives such as the excellent *Enciclopedia Italiana*. After the debacle of September 1943 he thought it honourable to stand by Mussolini and accepted the post of President of the Academy. In Florence he was seized by partisans and lynched as a collaborationist.

GOBETTI, Piero (1901–1926) in a very short life founded a tradition of liberal socialism that was to live after him in the movement known as Justice and Freedom. After contributing to Gramsci's *Ordine Nuovo*, in 1922 he founded a newspaper called *Rivoluzione Liberale* which became one of the most brilliant and corrosive anti-fascist organs until both the paper and its editor were destroyed by the fascists. Gobetti died in Paris of injuries received in Italy during a beating. His guiding idea was that the Risorgimento had failed: imposed by the leaders, it had not penetrated the national conscience, mainly because it had never been completed by a religious reform and a renewal of the economic structure. Gobetti preached the need to reconcile the rise of the masses with the maintenance of liberal practice, but he criticized the paternalistic and reformist approach of the social democrats.

GRAMSCI, Antonio (1891–1937) was the most powerful and original of Italian communist thinkers and the party's most prestigious leader before Togliatti. In Turin after World War I he led the movement to set up factory councils and founded the newspaper *Ordine Nuovo,* which became the organ of his group. One of the founders of the Italian Communist party, he became its secretary in 1924 after working in Moscow and Vienna on the secretariat of the Communist International. In 1926 he won the majority of the party to the ideas of *Ordine Nuovo* in opposition to the extremists but in 1927 he was arrested by the fascists and condemned to twenty years' imprisonment. He was released in 1933, a dying man, to end his life in a clinic. His notebooks, written in prison, are a prodigious part of communist literature. He saw fascism as the aggravation of the conflicts that had piled up in Italian society since the Risorgimento and he interpreted the religious question in Italy and the southern question as specific Italian versions of the peasant question. He preached the need for co-operation and unity between the industrial workers in the north and the peasants in the south, a doctrine which, by and large, has been accepted as the basis of Italian Communist thinking, though it has not always been acted upon and the discussion around it affects other groups besides the communist intelligentsia.

GRAZIANI, Rodolfo (1882–1955) commanded the Italian troops on the south front during the Abyssinian war, becoming Marshal of Italy and Viceroy of Ethiopia 1936–37. In World War II he commanded operations in North Africa but was removed after the retreat of 1941. After the armistice of September 1943 he rallied to Mussolini and became defence minister of the so-called Italian Social Republic. He was one of the very few fascist leaders to be condemned for collaboration by an Italian court but was released by an amnesty and became honorary president of the MSI or neo-fascist party.

MATTEOTTI, Giacomo (1885–1924) was a socialist deputy of the reformist trend and secretary of the party in 1924 when, in a famous speech to the Chamber, he bravely denounced the methods of violence and intimidation employed by the fascists to win the election. A few days later he was kidnapped and stabbed to death by fascist thugs headed by one Dumini. His body was discovered in a ditch two months later and the scandal shook the régime and would have unseated Mussolini but for the support of the King. The real instigators of the crime were never discovered. The assassins were virtually acquitted by a fascist court but the survivors were brought to justice in 1947. Matteotti became a hero and a symbol for Italian social democrats.

MUSSOLINI, Benito (1883–1945), Italy's fascist dictator, began his career as a revolutionary socialist imbued with the ideas of Sorel. He was editor of *Avanti* in 1914 but dropped the anti-militarist policy of the socialists in favour of Italian intervention in World War I. He was expelled from the party and (with financial help from France) founded his own paper, *Il Popolo d'Italia*. In March 1919, when post-war social agitation was at a peak, he founded the fascist movement (later converted into the fascist party), which owed its initial success to Mussolini's brilliant demagogy and his ability to appear all things to all men, thus attracting malcontents from many social strata. The movement became a crusade against the socialists. The fascist squads were employed to destroy the workers' organizations and Mussolini gained the financial and moral support of conservatives not only in the business world and among the landowners, but in the Church.

In October 1922, after the fascist march on Rome, King Victor Emmanuel III invited him to form a government. In two years he converted his government into a régime, after overcoming, with the King's help, the crisis brought on by the murder of Matteotti (q.v.). The dictatorship dates from Mussolini's speech of 3 January 1925 announcing an impending change. The opposition was outlawed, special courts were set up and the liberal freedoms suppressed. Mussolini was none the less favoured by the democracies, and his prestige and the cult of the 'Duce' became unassailable after the reconciliation with the Church perfected by the Lateran Treaties of February 1929. At first Mussolini sought the friendship of Britain and France with a view to arresting German expansion in Europe but he mistook the Stresa Agreement of 1935 for a free hand to carve himself an empire in Ethiopia. The Abyssinian war (1935–36) was successful and popular but it strained the country's resources and earned Italy the enmity of Britain and the censure of the League of Nations, whose sanctions united the Italians in resentment. Mussolini found himself forced into the alliance with Germany and the 'brutal friendship' with Hitler that was to be his undoing. The decline started with his participation in the Spanish civil war, which brought Italy no diplomatic advantage and cost the country dear. In 1940 Mussolini was not ready for a European war but the imminent collapse of France caused him to declare war on 10 June lest Hitler should dictate the peace without him.

Mussolini had replaced the King as Supreme Commander of the armed forces but his conduct of the war was disastrous. The Italians lost Abyssinia, took a beating in Greece and were chased out of North Africa. Sicily was occupied by the Allies. On 24 July 1943 the Fascist Grand Council voted Mussolini out of the supreme command and next day the King removed him from the government and had him arrested on the royal doorstep. Shortly after the armistice of September 1943 he was rescued from the Gran Sasso by a German commando and dispatched by Hitler to head the government of the fascist republic in northern Italy. At Salò he was not so much Hitler's puppet as his prisoner. In April 1945 he tried to come to terms with the Liberation Committee but his offer was repulsed. While escaping to the frontier he was intercepted by partisans and executed after a summary trial.

ROSSELLI, Carlo (1899–1937), radical anti-fascist leader, was a pupil of Salvemini with whom he founded the clandestine anti-fascist paper *Non Mollare*. When the persecutions started in 1925 he organized the expatriation of numerous political leaders, and was confined at Lipari for helping Turati to escape. He escaped from Lipari in 1929 with Lussu and F. Nitti and in Paris he founded the movement called Justice and Freedom, based on the attempt to harmonize Marxist doctrine with liberal democracy. The movement was active inside Italy. Rosselli was wounded in action during the Spanish civil war and while convalescing in France he was murdered, together with his brother Nello, by French fascists acting for Mussolini.

SALVEMINI, Gaetano (1873–1957) was Italy's most distinguished historian on the positivist side (in contrast to the idealism of Croce and Gentile). He was also one of the most vigorous and original of the *meridionalisti* or southern reformers. From his chair in the university of Florence and from his newspaper *L'Unità* (1911–20) he wielded a unique influence on the young intellectuals who were to distinguish themselves in the struggle against fascism. In 1925 he was arrested for running a clandestine anti-fascist paper, *Non Mollare* (Don't Yield); he emigrated and eventually settled in the United States, where he taught the history of Italian civilization at Harvard from 1933 to 1948. The movement for Justice and Freedom, and later the Action Party, were founded by his disciples among the radical anti-fascist expatriates.

SERRATI, Giacinto Menotti (1876–1926) was a leader of the maximalist trend in the Socialist party in conflict with Turati. He opposed Italian intervention in World War I and succeeded Mussolini as editor of *Avanti* in 1914. In 1917 he was imprisoned for his part in the rising at Turin. He jealously guarded the independence of the Socialist party and resented interference from Moscow, but when the conflict with the fascists became tragic he set up a faction to join the Third International. In 1924 this group fused with the Italian Communist party.

STURZO, Luigi (1871–1959), Sicilian priest and outstanding leader of the early Christian Democrat movement before World War I. In 1919 he founded the Popular party, the first catholic political party in Italy to be tolerated by the Pope. Sturzo was particularly interested in the theory and practice of local government – at one time he was mayor of Caltagirone – and believed in the merits of administrative decentralization. To some extent he succeeded in incorporating his ideas into the body of catholic social doctrine. In the elections of 1919 and 1920 the Popular party attracted a large catholic vote and might have been used to block the fascists, but in 1921 Sturzo refused to collaborate with Giolitti, possibly because the latter's fiscal programme would have damaged ecclesiastical interests and so deprived Sturzo of the always uncertain support of the Church. He lost this completely in 1923 when he tried to make the Popular party, which had several members in Mussolini's government, go into opposition. Since the Church had decided to support Mussolini, Sturzo's position became untenable. He resigned the secretaryship of the party and went into exile in 1924. In London, and after 1940 in New York, he kept up his opposition to fascism and published various books on politics, sociology and religion. He returned in 1946 but his last years were clouded by a futile newspaper polemic against state industry.

TURATI, Filippo (1857–1932) was leader of the reformist wing of the Italian Socialist party, which he helped to found in 1892. He sought to reconcile the workers' movement with the tenets of liberal democracy and was instrumental in winning the support of the middle-class intellectuals. He was more sensitive to the interests of the industrial working-class élite than to those of the peasants, whom he tended to consider reactionaries. While his faction was in control of the party he came to a working understanding with Giolitti but would not enter the government. During the troubles of 1920–22 the reformists lost control and Turati saw too late that under the threat of fascism the Socialists' first interest was to save the democratic bourgeois state. In 1922 he broke with the PSI to found a social democratic party (PSU), but in exile after 1926 he worked for the reunification of the Italian socialists.

CONTEMPORARY ITALY

AMENDOLA, Giorgio. Communist. Leads a trend in the Communist party in favour of bringing the party into government in a broad coalition with the Socialists and the Christian Democrats.

BADOGLIO, Pietro (1871–1956), Marshal of Italy. In World War I he was responsible for the successful attack on Monte Sabotino in August 1916 and became deputy chief of staff to Diaz. In 1918 he conducted the armistice preliminaries and signed the armistice for Italy. Governor-general of Libya (1928–33), in 1935 he was appointed commander-in-chief of operations in Abyssinia, concluding the campaign so rapidly as to provide German military experts with a text for the blitzkrieg. Chief of Staff at the outbreak of World War II, he resigned after the Italian defeat in Greece, for which he was blamed mainly because he had disapproved the campaign. On 25 July 1943 King Victor Emmanuel sent for him to form a government after the deposition of Mussolini. On 3 September 1943 he concluded the short armistice signed at Cassibile but was unable or unwilling to hold Rome open for the Allies and when these announced Italy's unconditional surrender on 8 September Badoglio joined the royal party on the flight to Pescara, leaving the city defenceless and the army without intelligible orders. At Brindisi, behind the Allied lines, his government of officials failed to obtain political support from the anti-fascist leaders who opposed the monarchy, but in March 1944 Togliatti arrived from the USSR to bring him the unexpected support of the Communists, who entered the government. This lasted until the liberation of Rome in June 1944. Badoglio's conduct in the period between 25 July and 8 September 1943 has been the subject of much polemical literature.

BERLINGUER, Enrico. One of the younger leaders of the PCI (Communist party). He is not committed to any particular alliance but favours getting the party into government within the present parliamentary system.

COLOMBO, Emilio (b. 1920). Christian Democrat politician of the moderate centre (Dorothean) faction. Has been minister of the Treasury in all the editions of the left-centre coalition. Working in close co-operation with the governor of the Bank of Italy, Guido Carli, his policy has been to keep a close check on the balance of payments and on the latent inflation, steering Italy out of the brief but alarming recession of 1963–64.

DE GASPERI, Alcide (1881–1954) was leader of the Christian Democrat party and prime minister (1946–53) during the difficult years of moral and material rehabilitation after World War II. He was born in the

Trentino under Austrian rule and sat in the Vienna parliament until 1918. In 1919 he was among the founders of the Popular party and succeeded Luigi Sturzo as its leader in 1923. Imprisoned by the fascists for four years, he spent the rest of the dictatorship as a political refugee in the Vatican. In 1943 he took a leading part in reorganizing the Catholic party (now called Christian Democracy) and soon became its undisputed leader. His experience as foreign minister during the humiliating peace negotiations of 1945–47 influenced his political thinking. His foreign policy was geared to restore Italy to a place of esteem among the western powers, if necessary at the cost of accepting United States hegemony. He led Italy into NATO with some reluctance and always hoped that some form of European federation could emerge as a third force between the USA and USSR. In home affairs he was a liberal catholic and believed in co-operation with the other democratic parties. His governments were all coalition ministries (first with the anti-fascist parties and later with the centre parties only) even after the Christian Democrats obtained an absolute majority in the Chamber. He always tried to keep the catholic integrationalists under control lest their intransigence should provoke the formation of an anticlerical front. But he was only partially successful in curbing clerical interference in politics and made little or no attempt to restrain the greed and corruption of the party bureaucrats and their clientèles. After the election of 1953 he was unable to re-form a coalition government and his last months were embittered by internal quarrels among the Christian Democrats.

DOLCI, Danilo, writer and social reformer, is probably better known outside Italy than at home, where a conspiracy of silence alternating with legal persecution (for libel, subversion and the like) tends to keep the public ignorant or misinformed about his work. For fifteen years he and his workers have been active in the poorest and worst Mafia-ridden areas of Sicily, trying to create a psychological breakthrough in a traditional society to enable the people to stand up to the Mafia and shape their own future. His books, *Waste, To Feed the Hungry* etc. have a wider circulation in English than in Italian.

FANFANI, Amintore (b. 1908), senior Christian Democrat politician, was considered a catholic integrationalist when he succeeded De Gasperi as party secretary in 1954. In 1958 he headed a two-party coalition government with the Social Democrats, but his personal inclination for a wider 'opening to the left' brought him the hostility of his own right wing. His government was brought down by 'snipers' and some of his former friends set up a new faction – the Dorotheans – to oppose him. In July 1960 he was back in government with a four-party coalition which was to prepare the way for the entry of the Nenni Socialists, and in February 1962 Fanfani formed the first left-centre government supported by, but not including, the PSI. The government lasted until the election of 1963 but when the left-centre coalition proper was finally set up Fanfani was no longer indicated by his own party for the premiership. He became foreign minister (1965–68) under Aldo Moro, becoming president of the United Nations XX Assembly. In June 1968 he was elected president of the Senate.

GRONCHI, Giovanni (b. 1887) succeeded Einaudi as second President of the Italian Republic (1955–62). A former catholic trade unionist, he represented a moderate left trend among the Christian Democrats. He was president of the Chamber 1948–55, when he was elected President of the Republic with the votes of the left, who ran him as a rival to his own party's official candidate. His presidential address calling for a more active social policy caused momentary alarm in business quarters and in the U.S. embassy. Believing that the President should take an active role in foreign policy, he encouraged some not very successful attempts to make Italy's voice heard as a mediator between East and West and to develop a special relationship with the Arab world. During his presidency, thanks partly to his influence, the Constitutional court was set up with the task of invalidating sentences passed in the courts in virtue of fascist police laws or other legislation contrary to the spirit of the constitution.

INGRAO, Pietro. Communist. Belongs to the generation of PCI leaders who have not experienced exile in the USSR. He leads a trend which is in favour of building up an alliance with the Catholic Left.

LEVI, Carlo (b. 1902), writer and painter, was sent by the fascists to the *confino* in Lucania, where his experience of a primitive peasant culture supplied him with the material for his book *Christ Stopped at Eboli*. This book, published in 1945, was fundamental in bringing the south and its problems to the attention both of intellectuals and of the general public. Levi's painting, like his writing, has often been inspired by the plight of the southern peasants. He ranks with Silone and the poet Rocco Scodellaro as one of the great instigators of a new attitude towards the south.

LONGO, Luigi (b. 1900), succeeded Togliatti as secretary-general and leader of the Italian Communist Party in 1964. He is the party's most distinguished military chief; was Inspector General for the Komintern of the International Brigades in Spain during the Civil War and later commanded the Garibaldi Brigades in Italy during the partisan struggle. As leader of the PCI he sticks to the line traced by Togliatti and although he censured the Russian intervention in Czechoslovakia in 1968, he is unlikely to lead the PCI into a breach with Moscow.

MATTEI, Enrico (1906-1962) played a fundamental part in bringing Italy to the point of industrial take-off leading on to the first post-war boom (1959-62). He was a man of extraordinary energy and singleness of mind. During the partisan struggle he commanded the catholic formations, representing them in the Liberation Committee for the north. In 1945 he was appointed commissioner to wind up the old state oil prospecting company AGIP but, after striking gas in the Po Valley in 1946, he made AGIP the corner-stone of a big state oil concern, ENI (1953). In his hands ENI became an instrument to shape the country's economic and foreign policy according to his views. His aim was to mop up unemployment, develop the south and promote Italy's economic penetration overseas, in Africa particularly but also in the USSR. His attitude was highly polemical towards the private sector and towards United States influence on Italian affairs. His own influence on Italian politics between 1958 and 1962 was very considerable.

MORO, Aldo (b. 1916), Christian Democrat politician of the centre left, was party secretary (1958-63) and succeeded in persuading the party to accept the principle of a coalition with the Socialists and the Social Democrats – the so-called 'Opening to the Left'. Between 1963 and 1968 he headed four successive governments based on this coalition. His position in the party is somewhat to the left of the dominant centre group known as the Dorotheans.

NENNI, Pietro (b. 1891), veteran leader of the Italian Socialist Party. For several years after the Liberation Nenni continued to favour the close alliance with the Communist party built up during the struggle against fascism but his faith in the creed of the unity of the working classes and his admiration of the Soviet Union as the incarnation of socialism were shaken by the events of the fifties; after the suppression of the Hungarian

196

rising he became completely converted to the theory and practice of western parliamentary democracy. Henceforth his aim was to lead the Socialists into government in a broad alliance with the democratic parties of the left centre. It took him six years to convince the other parties of his sincerity and even longer to convert the majority of his own party to his views, but the so-called Opening to the Left was achieved at last in 1963 when Nenni became Deputy Prime Minister in a government headed by the Christian Democrat Aldo Moro. Subsequently, in a later version of the coalition, he became Foreign Minister, a post he had occupied briefly twenty years earlier in a postwar coalition government under De Gasperi. The left-centre coalition broke down after the election of 1968 and shortly afterwards the ephemeral reunification of the Socialist and Social Democratic parties which Nenni had pursued since 1955 (and achieved in 1966), as a necessary corollary to his left-centre policy, came to an end. Since then Nenni's position in his own party has been seriously undermined and although his personal prestige and popularity are still considerable, he no longer controls the party's leaders.

PARRI, Ferruccio (b. 1890) was a militant anti-fascist and one of the founders of the Action party, which inherited the ideas and the programme of the movement for Justice and Freedom. During the partisan struggle he was one of the three main commanders of the volunteer corps in northern Italy, enjoying immense prestige. From June to November 1945 he was prime minister of the first postwar government to represent the Resistance, but his programme of structural reforms alarmed the Liberals while the Socialists and Communists failed or did not care to see that his downfall would be the end of any attempt to alter the power structure of the old fascist and pre-fascist establishment. Later he was made a life senator and his sympathies today centre on the extreme left.

RUMOR, Mariano (b. 1915), Christian Democrat politician of the moderate centre (the large faction known as the Dorotheans), was party secretary during the first edition of the left-centre coalition (1963–68) and took over as prime minister in December 1968 when the coalition, which had broken down after the general election of that spring, was re-formed. In the spring of 1969 the coalition again broke down (owing to a split between the Socialists and Social Democrats) and Rumor became prime minister of an all-Christian Democrat government geared to steer the country towards yet another revival of the centre-left coalition.

SARAGAT, Giuseppe (b. 1899), President of the Republic since December 1964. Originally a doctrinaire Marxist, he is said to have drafted the text of the alliance between the Italian Socialist and Communist parties in exile in 1934. In 1947 he promoted the big socialist split and led the Social Democrats to set themselves up as a separate party with an anti-communist platform. During the fifties he led this party into several coalition governments of the Centre with the Christian Democrats and the Liberals. Later he embraced the policy of the Opening to the Left (which brought the Nenni Socialists into government and excluded the Liberals) but he was reluctant to sanction any loss of autonomy for the Social Democrats, which would follow their reunification with the Socialists. The reunification itself could only be achieved after Saragat had been elected to the presidency of the Republic and when, in April 1969, the Social Democrats again broke away from the Socialists, it was assumed that he had approved, if not actually inspired the breach. Both as a politician and as President of the Republic Saragat has always stood for close relations between Italy and the United States.

SFORZA, Carlo (1872–1952), was foreign minister under Giolitti (1920–21) and negotiated the Treaty of Rapallo, by which Italy made peace with Yugoslavia after abandoning Fiume. He resigned from the post of ambassador in Paris when Mussolini came to power in 1922 and remained in exile during the dictatorship, principally in the United States, where he published numerous books in English against fascism and nationalism and in favour of European federation. He returned to Italy in October 1943 thanks to American pressures and against the wishes of Churchill, who disliked his republican ideas. Sforza was among those who tried to persuade Victor Emmanuel III to abdicate. As foreign minister under De Gasperi (February 1947–July 1951) he took a leading part in persuading his chief to accept the implications of Marshall Aid and to join NATO. Count Sforza is probably one of the principal architects of the special relationship between Italy and the USA.

SILONE, Ignazio (b. 1900), pseudonym of Secondo Tranquilli. A founding member of the Italian Communist Party, which he represented at various international conferences in Moscow. During the early years of fascism he took part in clandestine activity, but left the country in 1928. In exile in Switzerland he produced his two most famous novels, *Fontamara* (1930) and *Bread and Wine* (1937). Disgusted with the cruelty and intolerance of the Stalinists, he left the Communist party to join the PSI in exile. He was a deputy in the Constituent Assembly in 1945–47.

TOGLIATTI, Palmiro (1893–1964) was a founder and later the charismatic leader of the Italian Communist Party. In exile in the USSR during fascism he became Secretary of the Comintern and advocated the Popular Front policy of alliance with the Socialists. In April 1944, when Italy was still a theatre of war and Stalin had agreed to the division of Europe into an eastern and a western zone of influence, Togliatti returned to Italy to persuade the Communists in the south to drop their opposition to the monarchy and join the government. Henceforth, though he could not admit it, his actions were governed by the premise that a Communist revolution in Italy (violent or not) was impossible without upsetting the international equilibrium and therefore disturbing the USSR, whose interests, in the last analysis, he identified with those of the PCI. He kept the party in government until 1947 when, to appease the catholics, he voted for the incorporation of the Lateran Treaty in the constitution of the Republic. His policy in opposition was to make the PCI as broad a party as possible with small regard for the doctrinal orthodoxy of its members and with the ultimate aim of getting back into government through its parliamentary strength and its influence in local government. In the breach between the USSR and China he was basicly closer to Moscow than to Pekin although he claimed to have been one of the originators of the doctrine of the many (national) roads to socialism. His spiritual testament, written at Yalta a few days before he died, enjoined the Communists to remain united in diversity.

Index

Numbers in italic refer to illustrations

Iran, 144
Iron Curtain, the, 126
Isonzo, 66
Istituto Mobiliare Italiano (IMI), 140
Istria, 63, 68, 69, 131
Italian Academy, 95
Ivrea, 170

JACINI, Stefano, 17
Jacobins, 90
Jesuits, 13, 23, 170
Jews, 101, 120, 124
John XXIII, Pope, 63, *106*, 151, 172
Julian Alps, 63
justice, administration of, 160, 162,
   172
'Justice and Freedom', 93, 99, 116

KENNEDY, John F., 151
Keynes, J. M., 72, 82

LABOUR CHAMBERS, 36
Labriola, Antonio (*see* Who's Who,
   p. 186), 37, 57, 98
Lampedusa, Giuseppe, Prince of, 42,
   168
land reform, 138
La Pira, Giorgio, 121, 144
Lateran Pacts, the, 96, 124, 126
Latina, 158
Latin America, 130
Laval, Pierre, 98
League for the Defence of Freedom,
   39
League of Nations, 78, 98
Leghorn, Socialist Congress at, 75, 76
Lenin, V. I., 73, 75
Leo XIII, Pope, 40
Leopard, The (Lampedusa), *105*, 168
Levi, Carlo (*see* Who's Who, p. 195)
Libya, 47, 133, 144
Libyan War, 42, 47–8, 57, 58, 60, 62,
   97
Liguria, 88
Lloyd George, David, 71, 72
Lombardi, Riccardo, 154

Lombards, the, 8
Lombardy, 35, 102, 120
London, 36, 151; Treaty of, 63, 64,
   65, 68, 69, 70, 71
Longo, Luigi (*see* Who's Who, p. 196),
   55, 116
Lorenzo, General de, 154, 155
Lucania, 159
Luce, Clare Booth, 142, 146
Lumigiana, 33

MACHIAVELLI, Niccolo, 9, 10, 11, 172
Mack Smith, Prof., Denis, 18, 90
Madrid, 13
Mafia, 13, 26, 122, 139, 157, 168, 169,
   170
Magyars, 45
Malaparte, Curzio, 92
Malatesta, Errico, 83
Manfredi, Nino, 171
Marches, the, 58
Marcuse, Herbert, 164
Maremma, 138
Marinetti, Filippo, 58
Maritime Alps, 133
Marshall Aid, 134, 135, 137, 146
Martino, Gaetano, 152
Marx, Karl, 59, 121
Marxism, 36, 37, 38, 83, 127, 164, 167
Marzotto, 170
Massawa, 30
Mastroianni, Marcello, 171
Mattei, Enrico (*see* Who's Who,
   p. 196), *56*, 116, 142, 143, 144, 145,
   147, 152, 162
Matteotti, Giacomo (*see* Who's Who,
   p. 189), 85, 91, 97
Mazzini, Giuseppe (*see* Who's Who,
   p. 185), 25, 26, 27, 29, 36, 39, 45,
   49, 71, 89, 90
Menelik, Negus, 31
Meridionalisti, 44
Messaggero, Il, 29, 59
Messina, 46, 152
Metanopoli, 171
Metaponto, 156

Milan, 32, 33, 80, 82, 97, 120;
socialism in, 37, 76; unrest in, 39,
64, 73, 102, 162
Milazzo, Silvio, 151, 168
Minghetti, Marco, 17, 27
monarchy, role of, 18
Monicelli, Mario, 172
Montecatini, 28, 143
Monte Nevoso, 69
Moors, the, 8, 9
Morandi, Rodolfo, 126
Moro, Aldo (*see* Who's Who, p. 196),
150, 151, 153, 154
Morocco, 47
Mosca, Gaetano, 18
Moscow, 76, 82, 92, 131
motor industry, 163
Movimento Sociale Italiana (MSI), 150
music, 47
Mussolini, Benito (*see* Who's Who,
p. 189), *53, 54*, 61, 64, 69, 87, 89 *ff.*,
115; rise of, 57, 59, 62, 75;
foundation of fascist movement,
77–8, 79, 82, 84, 87–8; and the
Church, *53*, 81–2, 95–7; World War
II, 100–2; fall of, 102–3

NAPLES, 12, 16, 31, 33, 75, 116, 122,
157
Napoleon, III, 26, 27, 29, 65
Nasser, President, 144
nationalist movement, 46
nationalists, 57, 87
NATO, 134, 135, 136, 145, 147
natural gas, 142
navy, the, 28, 134
Nazi party, 94, 124, 132
Nenni, Pietro (*see* Who's Who, p. 196),
56, 76, 87, 92, 126, 128, 149, 151,
153, 154
Neo-fascists, 150
Neolithic Age, 7
New Learning, the, 10
Nice, 100
Nicola, Enrico de, 91
Nicolson, Harold, 72

Nitti, Francesco, 86, 87, 134
non expedit (1874), 41
North Africa, 43, 47, 102

OECUMENICAL COUNCIL, 151
oil industry, 142, 144
Ojetti, Ugo, 92
Olivetti, 170
'Opening to the Left', the, 149, 150,
151
Ordine Nuovo, 75
Orlando, Vittorio, 69, 70, 71, 72, 86,
88, 91, 134
Ostrogoths, the, 8
Ottaviani, Cardinal, 148
Ouchy, Treaty of, 47

PADRE PIO, 121
Palermo, 21, 151, 168, 169
Papacy, the, 8, 9–10; and the
Bourbons, 20; and fascism, 96; and
politics, 41, 44, 63, 80–1, 123–4,
135–6, 146, 147–8
Papal States, 12
Pareto, 59
Paris, 72, 93, 132, 165; Commune, 36
Parliament, 24–6, 31, 64, 140, 145,
155, 156, 163, 164, 169; Giolitti and,
43, 44, 47, 48, 58, 62; Mussolini
and, 79, 80, 82, 87–8, 90–2; *see also*
Chamber of Deputies
Parri, Ferruccio (*see* Who's Who,
p. 197), 116, 159
Partito Communista Italiano (PCI), 147,
165
Partito Nazionale Fascista (PNF), 90
Partito Socialista Democratico Italiano
(PSDI), 154
Partito Socialista Italiana (PSI), 147,
149, 153
*Partito Socialista Italiano di Unità
Proletaria* (PSIUP), 154, 165
Paul VI, Pope, 23, 169
Peace Conference (1919), 71, 72, 81,
82
Pella, Giuseppe, 131

205

Schuman, Robert, 133, 135
Schuster, Cardinal, 97, 125
Segni, Antonio, 150, 153, 155
Sella, Quintino (*see* Who's Who,
  p. 187), 21, 22, 43
Senise, Carmine, 94
Serbia, 64, 69, 70, 71; *see also*
  Yugoslavia
Serrati, Giacinto Menotti (*see* Who's
  Who, p. 191), 67, 75, 76
*Servizio Informazione delle Forze
  Armate* (SIFAR), 155
Sforza, Count Carlo (*see* Who's Who,
  p. 198), 92, 133, 135, 136
Shell, 143
Ship, The (D'Annunzio), 45
Sicily, 8–9, 13, 20, 66, 127, 134, 151,
  168, 169; the Mafia and, 26, 122;
  economy of, 32–3, 158; sulphur
  mines, 38, *51*; catholicism in, 121–2;
  land reform in, 137–8
Signorie, 167
Silone, Ignazio (*see* Who's Who,
  p. 198)
Sinigaglia, Oscar, 141
Skorzeny, Otto, 115
Slavs, 84
Smyrna, 68
Social Democratic party, 128, 145
Socialist International, 62, 129
Socialist party, 37–8, 43, 64, 83–4, 87,
  88, 146; splits in, 57, 76–7; under
  fascism, 93; De Gasperi and, 123,
  125, 128–9; Nenni and, 149, 154
Somaliland, 133
Sonnino, Sidney, 39, 60, 61, 63, 64,
  70, 71, 72
Sordi, Alberto, 171, 172
Soviet, 75
Soviet Union, 98, 128, 130, 131
Spaak, Paul-Henri, 135
Spain, 9, 12, 13, 99
Spanish-American War, 39
Spanish Civil War, 93, 98, 99, 100
Spanish Inquisition, 12
Split, 86

Spoleto, Duke of, 101
Squadrismo, 84, 87
Stalin, Josef, 93, 149
Stampa, La, 29, 92, 162
steel industry, 83, 132, 143, 144
Stresa, 98
students' movement, *111*, 164, 165,
  166
Sturzo, Don Luigi (*see* Who's Who,
  p. 192), 80–1, 92, 96, 120
Sudan, 30
Suez, 144
suffrage, male, 48
Switzerland, 155
Syllabus of Errors, 23, 41
Syracuse, 121, 158

TAGLIAMENTO, 66
Tambroni, Fernando, 150
Taranto, 144, 158
Tenda, 133
Terni, 28
Terracini, Umberto, 76, 90
textile industry, 83
Third International, 76, 90
Third Reich, 132
Tito, Marshal, 101, 116, 117, 131
Togliatti, Palmiro (*see* Who's Who,
  p. 199), 76, 90, 92, 93, 126, 137
Tognazzi, Ugo, 171
Trasformismo, 24, 25, 44
Tre Venezie, 86
Trent, Council of, 89
Trentino, 30, 45, 60, 63, 65, 68, 132
Trento, 30, 46, 61, 123, 164
Treves, 67, 75
Trieste, 30, 45, 61, 63, 65, 69, 84, 127,
  131
Trotsky, Lev, 75, 93, 154
Truman, President, 133, 134, 137
Tunisia, 29, 30, 100, 101
Turati, Filippo (*see* Who's Who,
  p. 192), influence of, 37, 38, 39, 43;
  eclipse of, 57, 64, 67, 75, 92
Turin, 17, 33, 74, 102, 133, 162, 164,
  170